Best Practices for Therapy
Empirically Based Treatment Pro

Dear Mental Health Professional:

This protocol is part of the *Best Practices for Therapy* that is designed to provide mental health practitioners empirically based treatment programs. We have edited this series to be clear and user-friendly, yet comprehensive and step-by-step.

The series offers high quality, consistently formatted protocols that include everything you need to initiate and complete treatment. Each session is outlined in detail with its own agenda, client education materials, and skill-building interventions. Each session also provides sample instructions and therapist-client dialogues.

The therapist protocol you are using corresponds with an available client manual that is designed to be used concurrently. Your protocol has all the worksheets, homework assignments, in-session treatment exercises, and didactic material that is in the client manual. Also included are pre- and post-assessments, and an overall program evaluation. An appendix contains a treatment plan summary (now required by many managed care companies).

Ten *Best Practices for Therapy* protocols are currently available or in development. They include protocols for PTSD, GAD, OCD, panic disorder/agoraphobia, specific phobia, social phobia, depression, anger management, BPD, and eating disorders.

We wish you every success in using this program with your clients.

Sincerely,

Matthew McKay, Ph.D.
John Preston, Psy.D.
Carole Honeychurch, M.A.

OVERCOMING GENERALIZED ANXIETY DISORDER

■

A Relaxation, Cognitive
Restructuring, and
Exposure-Based Protocol
for the Treatment of GAD

John White, Ph.D.

BPT

Best Practices for Therapy

Empirically Based Treatment Protocols

Publisher's Note

This publication is designed to provide accurate and authoritative information in regard to the subject matter covered. It is sold with the understanding that the publisher is not engaged in rendering psychological, financial, legal, or other professional services. If expert assistance or counseling is needed, the services of a competent professional should be sought.

Distributed in the U.S.A. by Publishers Group West; in Canada by Raincoast Books; in Great Britain by Airlift Book Company, Ltd.; in South Africa by Real Books, Ltd.; in Australia by Boobook; and in New Zealand by Tandem Press.

The STAI on pages 90–92 and the "Percentile Ranks for Adults" on pages 94–95 are reprinted with permission from Consulting Psychologists Press, Inc.

Cover design by Poulson/Gluck Designs
Edited by Donna Long
Text design by Michele Waters

ISBN 1-57224-144-6 Paperback

New Harbinger Publications' Website address: www.newharbinger.com

01   00   99

10   9   8   7   6   5   4   3   2   1

First printing

Dedicated with love to my wife, Marcia,
my abiding source of pioneer spirit.

amor vincit omnia

Let Your Light Shine

Our deepest fear is not that we are inadequate.
Our deepest fear is that we are powerful beyond measure.

It is our light, not our darkness, that most frightens us.

We ask ourselves: who am I to be brilliant, gorgeous,
talented, and fabulous? Actually, who are we not to be?

You are a child of God. Your playing small does not serve the world.
There is nothing enlightened about shrinking so that other people
won't feel insecure around you.

You were born to manifest the glory of God that is within us.
It is not just in some of us; it is in everyone.

And as we let our light shine, we unconsciously give other people permission
to do the same. As we are liberated from our fear, our presence
automatically liberates others.

—Excerpt from Nelson Mandela's Inaugural Speech, South Africa, 1994

Contents

Acknowledgments

Writing is one of those solitary activities that gives you plenty of time to think about all the people who made it possible for you to do that writing. This is a short list of my favorites.

It has been my good fortune to have enjoyed personal study with Tim Beck and Rollo May. Not only are each of these men brilliant teachers, but their two books on anxiety have been among the most important of the twentieth century. Rollo's ideas in *The Meaning of Anxiety* and Tim's in *Anxiety Disorders and Phobias* are the very foundation from which I developed my own book. I want to express my deepest gratitude. My appreciation to Tim extends further to all the wonderful people he has trained who, in turn, have had a significant influence in my development as a cognitive therapist. These include Judy Beck, Cory Newman, Jackie Persons, Chris Padesky, Jesse Wright, and Judy Washington. Tim has personally initiated this feeling of extended family among cognitive therapists and it remains one of the most satisfying features of this approach for me.

I also want to thank the people at New Harbinger who put together this Best Practices series. Having already developed a fine reputation in self-help literature, they are now turning the same principles toward writing about therapy. These protocols seek to make clear and practical information available to clients and therapists so as to facilitate real change in people's lives. Simple on the face of it, perhaps, but this is actually an enormous responsibility for a writer to live up to. I'm truly glad that I had the support of New Harbinger all along the way. In particular I want to thank Matt McKay, John Preston, and Donna Long. I would like to acknowledge further support from Charles Spielberger and Robert Most of Mind Garden who graciously made available the State-Trait Anxiety Inventory for my use. I appreciate research assistance from Damaris Urizar and Steve Langley who brought wonderful sources to me.

What a pleasure it was to work with my illustrators, Ezra Eismont and Alex White (who is also my eleven-year-old son). Together they crafted their own narrative of overcoming anxiety using no words whatsoever. The fine art of cartooning was their means of spinning the illustrated story you find in the Client Manual. Pan (short for Panic) is a feisty little character who struggles session by session to overcome his anxiety. Not unlike many of us with our own anxiety issues, he is alternately brash and overwhelmed—generally reflecting the human condition, it seems to me. His pal, the coyote Socko (short for Socrates), is the only one who can really get through to Pan. Socko draws upon the ageless wisdom of the coyote to help Pan discover those ways out of his anxiety. Their adversary in the story is Anxietron himself, the slightly silly mechanical villain who every session comes up with new ways to go after Pan. From the very beginning of this project I keenly wanted my book to have visual appeal as well as its own wit and humor. After all, anxiety is serious enough, I figured. Why can't we have some fun with the therapy? The cartoons produced by Ezra and Alex went far beyond what I hoped for. I hope you like them, too.

And finally I want to express my gratitude to my clients who have worked with me in overcoming their anxiety. I've long believed that most of what we as therapists know we developed in direct experience with our clients. This is certainly true of me. Not only have I learned greatly during my twenty years of clinical work, but daily I have been touched by the small acts of courage I see as individuals deal with their anxiety more fully. In my writing I have tried to convey my sense of hope for your progress based upon the positive developments I've been privileged to see in the lives of people who have shared their work with me. I sincerely wish the best for your health and happiness as you overcome your anxiety through the therapy we are undertaking together.

Introduction

With this manual, you and I will be working together to offer therapy to people with generalized anxiety disorder using a treatment protocol derived from cognitive behavioral therapy. This is no small undertaking. The indisputable cornerstone for success in such an endeavor is the assurance that you have full opportunity to draw upon all of your clinical skills and personal aptitudes as a therapist. The resulting therapy experience must be regarded by both you and your client to be personally satisfying as well as clinically effective. Nothing less will do. Upon this foundation, certain clinical dimensions will be added. Some of these will likely be familiar to you, and you're encouraged to engage in these at a sophisticated level. Others may be newer to you, and I will explain the material in a way that is both accessible and practical.

The first task is to gain a deeper understanding of the person who experiences generalized anxiety disorder (GAD). While I necessarily start from the *DSM-IV* diagnosis (American Psychiatric Association 1994), by itself that is a rather flat description; in this manual I wish to offer a fuller and richer picture of this particular individual. The clinical framework is provided by cognitive behavioral therapy (CBT) and I will discuss and apply the leading methods of this integrative approach.

Finally, a few words about working together in therapy using a treatment protocol: while there has been a recent groundswell of activity in protocol treatment, I still prefer the original definition of "protocol" that comes from the Greeks and means "a table of contents crafted from sheets of papyrus glued together." In this light the protocol provided here serves as a table of contents for you and your client to bring together the best researched methods in support of your ongoing therapy so your client can overcome her anxiety. (Throughout this manual, references to clients will reflect both genders: the male pronoun is used in odd-numbered chapters, the female pronoun appears in even-numbered chapters and the Introduction. Clinical examples are provided from my therapy sessions with actual clients. Their names and all identifiers have been changed to assure their privacy.)

Overview of the Disorder

Major Clinical Features

Virtually everyone experiences anxiety at various times in their lives. Ours is a high-pressure society and anxiety is a natural reaction to the environment we've created for ourselves. For most people, when the immediate pressure subsides their intense feelings of anxiety will gradually settle down. At such times they may enjoy some measure of peace of mind, physical relaxation, and personal pleasure. These more settled periods can be seen as an opportunity for them to "charge their batteries" for the next occasion of high anxiety.

But for the person who experiences GAD, the high level of anxiety never really subsides (Craske et al. 1989). She remains on edge much of her day-to-day life. There is no time to charge her battery and she has too little peace of mind, relaxation, or pleasure. Wherever she goes she is accompanied by a continuing sense of worry and apprehension. If she tries to reduce her anxiety she may become even more frustrated because it seems so unshakable. Looking to the future often brings a sense of dread because the anxiety only seems to grow larger. As the name itself conveys, her anxiety is truly generalized and she is likely to feel trapped inside this condition in all aspects of her life.

According to the *DSM-IV* (see Works Cited), a person with GAD experiences the following five symptoms:

1. Excessive anxiety and worry (apprehensive expectation), occurring more days than not for at least six months, about a number of events or activities (such as work or school performance).

2. The person finds it difficult to control the anxiety.

3. The anxiety and worry are associated with three or more of the following six symptoms (with at least some symptoms present for more days than not for the past six months):

   restlessness or feeling keyed up or on edge
   being easily fatigued
   difficulty concentrating or mind going blank
   irritability
   muscle tension
   sleep disturbance (difficulty falling asleep or staying asleep, or restless unsatisfying sleep).

4. The symptoms are not caused by another anxiety disorder.

5. The anxiety, worry, or physical symptoms cause clinically significant distress or impairment in social, occupational, or other important areas of functioning.

6. The disturbance is not due to medication, a general medical condition, or mood disorders.

Etiology

There is an emerging recognition of a certain biological predisposition toward anxiety for those people who experience GAD. It seems their bodies are more likely to register restlessness, muscle tension, and a variety of sleep disturbances (Kagan et al.

1997). Think of it as a physical threshold that is set slightly lower for these individuals to develop anxiety. Reckoning with the biological origins of GAD serves to correct the stereotype that anxiety is "all in your head," as if an individual could simply get control and make it go away through willpower. After all, who can make biology go away? Understanding the physical basis of the disorder helps a person with GAD relieve a natural tendency to compare herself with others and feel bad because "I want to be like them." Those other people likely have their own thresholds for tendencies such as anger, shyness, substance use, or any of a growing range of psychological traits recognized to have a biological basis. Dealing with your own tendencies produces a better life experience than worrying about how you compare with others.

Does this mean that people with a predisposition toward anxiety will automatically develop GAD? Not at all. A number of factors are at work, including how one was raised as well as one's current life experience (Ekman and Davidson 1994). Did one or both parents experience anxiety, and if so what examples did they provide in dealing with it? Were there significant traumas that signaled to the child that the world is not a safe place? Whether GAD fully manifests is clearly affected by one's means of making a living, and how much satisfaction it provides compared to its downside pressures and demands. The potential for GAD is also very much influenced by the relationships one develops and maintains over a lifetime. To what extent do these provide comfort, stress, or some combination of both? These multiple factors determine whether anxiety breaks into the foreground, and whether it does so strongly enough to warrant a diagnosis of GAD.

A diagnosis of GAD means there was probably some type of predisposition toward anxiety that was then activated by pervasive patterns in childhood, work experience, and personal relationships (Lang 1985, 131–170). Therapy helps an individual learn better methods of dealing with these patterns as they emerge. No less important is providing the client with relaxation skills to gradually reduce the body's threshold for anxiety.

Prevalence

How common is GAD? What about the other anxiety disorders? Approximately 5.1 percent of the general population will experience GAD at some point in their lifetime (Hallowell 1997). This year 3.1 percent of Americans meet diagnostic criteria for GAD. That's over seven million people. And when you consider individuals who have a concurrent phobia or panic with GAD as a leading feature, the prevalence increases to 10 to 12 percent. This represents a larger proportion of the general population than those suffering from alcohol or drug abuse (Craske, Barlow, and O'Leary 1992).

Over the course of a lifetime at least one in four people—or some 65 million individuals—will meet the criteria for one or more of the psychological conditions called anxiety disorders (Hallowell 1997). Anxiety is an equal-opportunity condition. It occurs across all levels of socioeconomic status and professions and across a variety of racial and ethnic backgrounds. While women tend to show more anxiety disorders than men, men are catching up.

A recent survey of primary-care physicians in the United States reported that at least one-third of office visits were prompted by some form of anxiety. It outranks bad colds and bronchitis! All told, anxiety disorders account for 31.5 percent of total costs of psychiatric disorders in this country: it is therefore the number-one mental health problem in the United States (Slawsky 1997).

Essential Elements of This Treatment Approach

What Is Cognitive Behavioral Therapy (CBT)?

The cognitive part of CBT refers to the power of our beliefs. What we believe about ourselves, our world, and our future has a strong influence on what actually happens (Beck and Emery 1985). Much of what we believe in these areas is not in our direct awareness; it is so much a part of us that we assume it to be true and act accordingly. CBT therapy begins by bringing these kinds of beliefs out of the shadows and into full view. This way we can begin to determine which beliefs are strong and valuable parts of us that we want to sustain, and which beliefs may have had some kind of basis in the past and have outlived their usefulness.

The behavior part of CBT acknowledges that real change happens in our life only when we *do* things differently. There needs to be some kind of action that brings the new direction to life (Barlow 1993). If therapy consisted only of thinking and talking and talking and thinking, what would really change? Probably not enough to make clients feel substantially better. CBT is always looking for ways in which what has been learned by clients during the session can be translated into their day-to-day life. This way they have direct opportunity to see what works for them and what needs to be modified and tried again. CBT uses homework to give clients more opportunity to practice what they've learned from therapy in their daily experience. The central role of homework is one of the reasons that research shows over and over that CBT is among the best methods in therapeutic improvement. The more regularly clients apply what they've learned in therapy, the more effective therapy will be for them.

Central to CBT is what is called the collaborative relationship between the therapist and the client. This means that you and your client will be working as partners to get the best possible results (Beck 1995). The word "collaborate" derives from a Latin word meaning "to labor together." Because this is a partnership, your client should feel free to ask you wide-ranging questions about the treatment you are undertaking together. These methods are useful only to the extent that she fully understands what is intended. If there happen to be issues that you and she disagree on, it is vital that she feel comfortable to speak up. This would be an important area of discussion between you and your client, hopefully resulting in the kind of adjustments that would feel good to both of you as well as encouraging a deeper alliance between you and your client. Regarding homework, you will encourage your client and suggest the benefits to her, but obviously it is her ultimate choice how much she does and what it consists of. CBT finds this to be the best means of maintaining a therapeutic relationship that is supportive of real change while respectful of individual responsibility.

In some circles there are lively discussions about what CBT is and is not. If you are interested in a tongue-in-cheek debate of the "Top Ten Myths and Misconceptions about CBT," turn to appendix 2.

What Does CBT Have to Say about Anxiety?

The anxious person is unusually burdened by a stubborn set of beliefs that the world is a threatening place (Beck and Emery 1985). These feelings have often been reinforced by past experiences of trauma, and the individual may feel that it is necessary for her to remain vigilant against harm at all times. Her sense that her surroundings are dangerous is compounded by equally strong beliefs that she lacks the psychological skills or resources to deal with the demands at hand. No matter how hard she tries, her efforts are not sufficient to gain any sense of peace or satisfaction with herself. This is especially tragic because anxious people are often seen by others to be quite competent, but the truth of this remains invisible to the anxious individual.

In order for therapy to make a difference, the individual will need to open up and shed light on the beliefs that have imprisoned her (Foa and Kozak 1986). In what ways exactly is the world seen as dangerous, both now and in the past? What are the circumstances of threat and where are the possible conditions of security? She needs to have real experience in safe situations that allow her to meet the challenges that come her way. As she increases her recognition of her competence, the world gradually will seem more predictable and less threatening. Her practice of physical relaxation will address her chronic tension so she does not feel on guard all the time. And along with these physical changes will be emotional changes: she will be reexamining her relationships to favor those with mutual support and a shared sense of handling risk.

Basic Elements of This Manual

This manual provides everything you need to know in terms of preparing for the sessions and using the therapy time during the session. It's written with the expectation that you are a trained and experienced therapist and that you are bringing all of those skills into the clinical interaction with your client. But because treating GAD, working in a CBT model, and/or using a treatment protocol may be new approaches for you, this treatment guide offers practical skills as you develop your expertise in these areas.

Make sure to read the Client Manual before you start. This will provide you with a firsthand perspective into this portion of your client's therapy experience. In particular, you need to be aware of how she is using the manual during the periods between sessions with you. Because the Client Manual is truly a separate book from this one, it would be a good idea if you were familiar with it.

Through a collaborative relationship with you, your client will learn certain skills that have been shown to be highly effective in helping people overcome GAD. Your understanding and support help give your client the confidence to try these new experiences.

New Skills

Scheduling worry time: This is a simple method of asking the client to select a worthwhile topic associated with her worry and committing some time to it.

Relaxation: Daily practice brings physical relief from anxiety and provides a platform for the emotional and mental changes to come. Time spent developing skills for relaxation will pay off in the client's openness and willingness to accept other interventions later.

Risk assessment: The client begins to see where she may over-respond to current situations on the basis of damage done by old threats. Hopefully, she will recognize there can be a variety of ways of seeing a situation and she is not obliged to always assume as true the most frightening view.

Problem solving: For there to be real gains in overcoming anxiety, your client needs to feel a greater sense of confidence in her ability to solve life problems that come her way. This develops in part by learning and practicing one simple method of dealing with problems, which will be outlined in session 5.

Worry exposure: This is the most effective means of reducing an anxious person's tendency to avoid problems. In a humane and supportive manner the individual is encouraged to confront rather than avoid the sources of threat.

Reducing safety behaviors: By slowly dispensing with her safety behaviors, your client can test where there remains a real need for her concern and where she can afford to relax.

Thought-stopping: When anxious thoughts appear, your client can learn to listen to them, challenge them, or stop them. She can maintain a significant influence on her overall mental state based upon how she responds to the thoughts.

Revising core beliefs: Over the course of therapy your client will learn to recognize her core beliefs about herself, her world, and her future. Here she learns to test the old rules that supported her anxiety and develop alternate core beliefs that better reinforce what she now wants from her life.

Relapse prevention: Will future anxiety triggers lead to a full relapse of GAD? The gains of a successful treatment need to be consolidated in such a way that they can be effectively used by the client in the future.

Research

To Treat or Not to Treat?

The majority of people experiencing GAD do *not* seek treatment (Hallowell 1997). They tend to regard themselves as chronic worriers and assume that nothing can really help them. By contrast, people who experience panic are roughly four times more likely to pursue treatment than people with GAD, probably due to the dramatic nature of a panic attack. Untreated, GAD tends to last longer than panic disorder and impact a greater portion of a person's life.

This manual brings together the most successful and effective methods of treating GAD (Brown, Hertz, and Barlow 1992). When people with GAD complete this type of manual-based treatment, 70 percent of them show marked improvement (Craske, Barlow, and O'Leary 1992). Their physical symptoms have decreased, they show much less tendency to worry (Blowers, Cobb, and Matthews 1987), and they find greater enjoyment in their daily lives (Lindsay et al. 1987). At conclusion of treatment they no longer meet the criteria for GAD (Butler et al. 1991). These therapeutic gains are still maintained at a six-month follow-up and a decrease in the use of medication is noted.

Protocol versus Nondirected Therapy

A protocol such as this brings together the best proven techniques for overcoming GAD (Barlow, Rapee, and Brown 1992). The methods have been refined and researched to establish what is most useful to people. You have the opportunity to benefit from this accumulated experience.

While nondirected therapy is indicated in some clinical situations, it is not structured to include the main tools that reduce GAD (Hollon and Beck 1993, 428–466). Sessions do not typically include the teaching of skills, and the time between sessions does not usually involve homework. But with protocol therapy, skill-building and the use of homework allows you to employ the best available methods to reduce your client's GAD. Naturally you will use these skills in a way that is tailored to your client's situation and flexible to her needs.

Duration of Treatment

On average, this treatment takes between ten and twelve sessions, each of which is usually scheduled weekly (Barlow, Rapee, and Brown 1992). Depending upon individual progress, the pace may go faster or slower. Usually the individual sessions are completed in one week. You and your client will, of course, make adjustments as necessary. Those sessions that sometimes warrant extension to a second week are: Relaxation (session 2), Worry Exposure (session 5), and/or Revising Core Beliefs (session 8). This depends on your client's needs at the time and how she can best make progress in overcoming her anxiety.

Assessment

During the first session you will conduct a clinical interview with your client to determine if there is a diagnosis of GAD. The *DSM-IV* profile of the condition has been provided earlier, in the section entitled "Major Clinical Features." As you are probably aware, these criteria are essentially a list of symptoms and do not, in and of themselves, comprise a full diagnostic investigation. Instead, on the basis of your therapeutic training, you will obtain the complete range of clinical data necessary to make a thorough diagnosis. This would include the client's subjective descriptions of her current life, with an exploration of personal strengths as well as her view of her weaknesses or problems. There would need to be a full history to gauge the developmental profile of anxiety over her lifetime, with particular attention to any formative trauma that might be linked to her anxiety. Family and medical background are obviously necessary in light of anxiety's demonstrated genetic and physiological associations (including drug and alcohol effects, obviously). In short, you will make sufficient investigation to rule in or rule out competing conditions so there can be a meaningful differential diagnosis regarding GAD.

Self-Rating Scales

As part of the diagnostic process the client will be asked to take the State Trait Anxiety Inventory (STAI) between sessions one and two (Spielberger 1983). It doesn't involve more than ten minutes—for forty questions—and provides another perspective on the client's experience of her anxiety. It allows her to obtain an objective measure of her anxiety and, if she chooses, to see how her anxiety level compares to the general population. She will repeat measures at a midpoint in therapy (between sessions 4 and 5) and at the conclusion of therapy (between sessions 8 and 9). This gives her the opportunity to observe how her anxiety changes over the course of treatment.

You, too, can benefit from using the STAI. Depending upon your interests, you may also want to access the well-established research base for the test. At last count there were over thirty-three hundred citations for the STAI that provide norms and applications with a broad range of cultural and ethnic groups as well as various diagnostic categories (Spielberger 1989). You may also choose to use the test results as a formal outcome measure of treatment. Since managed-care companies and third-party payers are increasingly asking therapists to independently document the results of therapy, the STAI provides an outcome measure of high quality. The methods of interpreting the test appear in appendix 1.

Each session begins with a brief self-rating scale that allows the client to rate her experiences pertaining to the topic addressed in that session. There are two benefits to this: it brings to light those tendencies on the client's part that serve to increase her anxiety, and it identifies her existing strengths for dealing with anxiety in a constructive manner. The client will complete the rating scale as a preview to her session with you and bring the results with her for mutual discussion. Individual items can also serve as target areas for specific change and provide comparison at a later time to see where progress is leading.

Specific Goals and Limitations of Treatment

The obvious goal in undertaking this treatment is to reduce anxiety sufficiently that the client no longer warrants a diagnosis of GAD. But that alone will likely not be enough of a goal to reach that outcome. A process of change can proceed only so far through a desire for reduction in anxiety. Therapy for overcoming GAD will be stronger if you and your client agree about what kinds of positive goals she wants in her life over the course of treatment (Bourne 1995). Such goals might include more pleasurable time spent with her children, better fitness to deal with her physical stress, or the confidence to speak up in a work setting without silently second-guessing herself. Positive goals such as these make the treatment unique for each individual. The better your client can focus on these goals, the more likely she is to stay with therapy and push ahead with homework even when she is temporarily discouraged and experiencing feelings of frustration.

The main limitation to the effectiveness of treatment occurs when there are significant co-morbid conditions existing with GAD. For example, if a client experiences acute posttraumatic stress disorder superimposed on GAD, it will be difficult to bracket off the PTSD and treat the GAD alone. Or there may be a drug or alcohol addiction that undercuts the client's ability to focus her energies and tolerate the discomfort of treating the GAD. Perhaps you will see a significant personality disorder, such as borderline, that ushers in labile affect, self-destructive behaviors that would reduce the effectiveness of treating the GAD. In the case of PTSD, substance abuse, and/or borderline personality, it would be necessary to stabilize these conditions first. Once gains had been made and a collaborative relationship is established between you and the client, together you might then consider treatment of the anxiety.

Agenda Setting

Opening the Session

During the first ten to fifteen minutes of the session you'll reconnect with your client. This includes her description of how she's feeling at the time of the session (with particular attention to anxiety) and a discussion of her personally significant events during the week. Together you'll review the homework, paying special attention to results that are new or unexpected. Likewise, you and she will consider the record she has made of her anxiety experiences throughout the week as well as unresolved issues that remain.

Exploring a New Skill

Approximately half the session is used to help the client learn a new therapy skill. In a time-limited therapy world, this is a significant commitment. Time is apportioned in order to cover the skill in some depth.

The particular sequence of skills outlined in this manual has been shown over and over to be a strong ally in overcoming GAD; there is indisputable value in helping the client learn and master each of these skills. The CBT therapist needs to be able to engage with the client in such a way that this learning experience has warmth, interest, and relevance. Therapy will probably fail if the client feels the skills are forced, impersonal, or disconnected from what she really needs. It will probably also fail if the client senses the therapist does not truly believe in the validity of what she is presenting.

The new skills are best taught when the therapist is able to explain the material in ways that mesh with the client's learning style and draw upon a range of her personal experiences from the therapy sessions so far. A dialogue is more productive than a lecture. Questions and answers are exchanged as both client and therapist figure out how to make the best fit of the new skill into the client's life experience.

Conclusion

The final ten to fifteen minutes in each session will be spent in drawing the session to a close. Unresolved issues, particularly regarding anxiety, are addressed. Both therapist and client will anticipate worry issues that may arise during the week and how these can be dealt with. Homework is planned and modified as needed. The session is summarized by both parties and the client provides feedback to the therapist about the therapeutic relationship and progress to date.

After Session

Shortly after the session the client reviews the new skill as described in her Client Manual. She should practice the new skill daily. This constitutes the larger portion of the client's homework. A troubleshooting section is included in each chapter of the Client Manual for common issues or questions that may come up.

The Daily Worry Record

The client is asked to make a weekly record of her anxiety. This consists of a Daily Worry Record (see session 1) and a Thought Record (see session 3). These two records will prove to be a valuable resource in the opening of each therapy session as you and the client review her anxiety experiences during the week.

Preview for the Next Session

Prior to the start of each new session, the client is asked to read a brief introduction to the material to come. Included in this preview is a ten-question self-assessment on the new topic. This is designed to orient the client toward the next stage in treatment and generate good clinical material for the upcoming session.

Homework

Your single most effective means of influencing your clients to do their homework is your personal experience of having done it yourself. Your clients will likely sense whether or not you've completed these procedures step-by-step as a client would. The next strongest predictor of success with homework will be making sure that you follow up on it each and every time it is undertaken (Persons 1989). Even if the client has not done the homework, the opportunity arises for a valuable discussion about the issues that got in the way and how these could be addressed in the planning of subsequent homework. Obviously, there is no point in shaming or blaming the client. But if you do not follow up on the homework, you communicate to the client that you don't truly consider it necessary to the therapy process and the client will likely stop the homework shortly thereafter.

Homework does not need to be completed perfectly. If that were to be the case each and every time, it would probably mean that the client is not risking or learning as much as she could (Zinbarg et al. 1992). Homework is intended to introduce a life experience that the client has not encountered before. The value, then, is the rich new mixture of feelings, thoughts, and actions that result. Over time and with practice the client learns additional life skills via the homework, and this is good. But there is no substitute for the client's personal and less-than-perfect experiences in the learning process; such experiences can be a vital contribution to the ongoing therapy.

How much time should be invested in homework? Let's start by acknowledging that everyone is busy and probably has too much to do. After all, these are anxious times, right? So the question of how much time the client can commit to homework will depend on how much she can set aside from everything else she is doing. Obviously, the more time she can devote to homework the greater benefit she'll get from the therapy. This is no different than learning any other new skill, such as playing a new sport, learning a musical instrument, or practicing a foreign language.

Your client will need up to an hour a day for the physical part of this treatment, which consists of relaxation and exercise. In the early weeks she will be learning relaxation techniques because it is so important for her to gain some physical relief from her anxiety (Roemer and Borkovec 1993). After several weeks of time-intensive practice with relaxation, she'll likely be feeling better and will possess more skills that allow her to relax quickly and effectively during her day-to-day life (McKay, Fanning, and Davis 1997). She can then adjust her hour-a-day commitment to include physical exercise or stretching as well as relaxation.

She'll also need up to an hour a day for the mental/emotional part of this treatment. There are many old habits that have been feeding her anxiety, and practicing new ways of relating to herself and to others takes time. People who are able to commit this kind of time to their progress almost always report that it was a satisfying experience.

Your client may look at these time estimates and feel that they are impossible. Does that mean that this therapy will do her no good and she should give up now? Hardly. People start where they are ready to start. If she is prepared to begin this therapy program, that is a good sign. Use whatever time is available to her. Perhaps as therapy progresses she will find herself able to commit more time. That would be great. Or maybe she'll just have to do the best she can for now. That would be fine, too. It's up to her.

It is vital in your therapeutic relationship with your client that she feel comfortable talking with you about her honest reactions to doing homework. If she has concerns or reservations about homework, this may reflect certain life patterns that led to her anxiety in the first place. It's all part of the therapeutic process. The client needs to feel that she can discuss these matters with you without her being criticized or made to feel ashamed. She also needs to see that you are not put off or daunted. Like anything else that arises in the therapeutic relationship, this is an opportunity for a greater sense of collaboration and mutual understanding.

Concurrent Pharmacologic Treatment

Many people with GAD are placed on medications by their primary-care physician. If your client is on medication as she starts this therapy program, I recommend that she not decrease her levels during treatment unless told to do so by her physician. She needs to maintain the benefit of medication while she is learning therapy skills. At the conclusion of this type of manual-based treatment, approximately 30 percent of people who are on medication are ready to decrease and eventually stop (Craske, Barlow, and O'Leary 1992). Suggest that she talk with her physician about these issues. You may want to ask her permission for your contacting the physician directly in order to coordinate treatment and medications.

Common Issues and Problems

Your Client's Attitude toward Using a Manual in Therapy

As with any other important feature of therapy, the client's attitude toward using a manual will closely mirror yours (Padesky and Greenberger 1995). If you have not already worked successfully with a manual, I suggest that you take yourself through this program week by week and perform all the tasks asked of the client. This gives you the best opportunity to determine if you feel that you will be offering a quality service to your clients. Besides, there's no better way to learn something than by doing it yourself. Pay close attention to your reactions and questions, as these will likely give you insight into what your clients experience. Make sure to do the homework so that you can see firsthand if it really makes a difference for you. Unless you personally believe that there is value in the homework, you'll have a difficult time convincing your client that it will really be of help to her.

Most therapists were not originally trained to use manuals in therapy; this is still a new development in our field. As with anything else that differs from what we are familiar with, you may have a variety of reactions to using a manual—perhaps partly interested and curious, maybe somewhat skeptical. If you've read this far, you're probably inclined to at least give it a try. You might think of this as a new opportunity for you to grow and develop in your work as a therapist. There is little doubt that the use of therapy manuals will adapt and evolve over the years as a result of our cumulative experience, and you have an opportunity to become a knowledgeable participant in that process.

Staying on Track

Part of the value of a manual is its influence on keeping the therapy on track. There is a natural tendency in dealing with anxiety for the client (and sometimes the therapist, too) to subtly avoid the sources of psychological threat (Clark 1989, 52–96). Therapist and client may talk about all kinds of clinical matters while managing to steer around the anxiety itself. A manual helps to keep the therapy focused on the presenting issue of anxiety (Borkovec et al. 1987). However, the therapist is responsible for making sure the refocusing is felt by the client to be useful and caring. If or when other topics arise, you can help the client find the relief she needs while also drawing a connection back to the main subject of anxiety. You can also make note of where in the therapeutic relationship anxiety arises or where it may be avoided. This becomes an in-the-moment opportunity to further explore the main clinical issue. If additional topics are to be dealt with in therapy, try to make sure there has first been some real headway in handling anxiety; remember that pursuing other topics can deflect attention away from anxiety.

Who Purchases the Manual for Your Client?

Therapists these days deal with enough complication in their professional lives from managed care and other bureaucratic red tape. For many, revenues are down and overhead is up. Therefore, I suggest that the therapist not be the one who purchases the Client Manual. In some settings it can be provided by a clinic or center, in others it can be made available by a third-party payor, while in others it can be acquired by the clients themselves. Therapists are advised to be creative and forward-thinking in making such arrangements.

Termination and Follow-up

CBT treatment of anxiety is based upon a recovery model rather than an aim for a cure. This acknowledges that because of a client's biological predisposition as well as her cumulative life experience, there will be a tendency for an individual who has once had GAD to experience at least some anxiety in the years to come. The long-term effectiveness of this treatment rests upon whether she can adequately deal with those future anxiety triggers and avert a new episode of GAD, versus a deterioration to a full relapse (Seligman 1991). The gains of a successful treatment for GAD need to be consolidated in such a way that they can be effectively used by the client in the future. For this reason, a key aspect of drawing this therapy to a close is helping the client prepare to apply these therapeutic lessons when she is on her own.

As you and your client reach the final sessions of this protocol, together you will be making an assessment of her anxiety symptoms as well as her overall progress. Depending upon the results, there will be three options in drawing this work to a close: "ready to finish," "ready to finish with a booster," or "need to continue" (for more information on these three options, see session 9). At whatever point their treatment concludes, clients are urged to integrate and maintain their therapy skills in day-to-day life. Each individual is asked to identify key skills that have been particularly useful to her, and together you can then make plans for her to regularly practice those skills after the conclusion of therapy. You should also ask clients to reflect upon the patterns of their anxiety and determine those early warning signs that signal when anxiety is beginning to build. Proper attention at these occasions can keep anxiety from escalating and perhaps relapsing to GAD. If the individual's own resources are not enough to curb the anxiety, this might be a good time for a follow-up session with you or another therapist to reinforce her ability to cope with the anxiety.

Session 1

Getting Started

Building an Initial Alliance

The essential task of the therapist in the first session is to build a therapeutic alliance. The ultimate success of the therapy depends upon the relationship between you and your client that begins to unfold from this first session onward. As you know from your clinical experience, clients need to feel heard and understood and need to believe that their therapist is genuinely interested in helping.

CBT describes this alliance as the collaborative relationship between you and your client and considers it the cornerstone of therapy. Given the nature of anxiety, the therapist can expect certain issues to arise in developing a collaborative relationship. An anxious person entering therapy will often want to know exactly what is expected from him and what he can expect from the therapist. The more you can address these expectations in a practical and friendly manner, the more your client will likely feel reassured. There may be a lot of questions from the client that, once again, are his attempt to determine whether working with you will feel safe. Answer the questions in a helpful and matter-of-fact way. To avoid responding to questions or to let long silences develop would obviously increase his anxiety and may lead him to break off from therapy. As you probably know from working with anxious clients, there is a tendency for their anxiety to be contagious and make you anxious. When you can comfortably handle these issues, you not only promote the collaborative relationship but model to the client how he can go about overcoming his own anxiety.

After introductions, opening questions such as, "How can I be of assistance to you?" begins a dialogue about the client's goals for therapy. Then it is useful to proceed directly to the client's history. There needs to be a collaborative assessment to determine whether a diagnosis of GAD is accurate and, if so, what treatment would be useful. Asking the client to describe his current problem and its history conveys your interest and concern—the purpose of history-taking is not only to obtain relevant information but to build rapport. Since clients often need to express strong feelings upon their first contact with a therapist, it is important in the first twenty to thirty minutes to let them tell their story in their own way. Be sure to listen carefully. While you may ask specific questions, such as suggesting he elaborate on what he is saying, you probably don't want to interrupt or redirect the flow of conversation.

In addition to telling his story during the first session, your client will likely be trying to determine whether he feels an empathic connection with you. To what extent does he sense that you understand his emotional experience with anxiety? Do you recognize his struggles as real, or do you minimize them as other people in his life might? Can you accept his frustration about not being able to effect change on his own, or do you think he has not been trying hard enough? Obviously, there is no way to manufacture these empathic responses on your part nor is there a formula by which to share them with your client. As you self-monitor while working with your clients, ask yourself about your emotional response to what they are saying. If you recognize that you feel concern and interest, this is the opening for building a genuinely empathic relationship with your client. Perhaps you will develop a specialty working with anxiety if this is a natural area of emotional understanding for you. If you find yourself having difficulty feeling concern and interest in your client, see if you can understand and adjust what is getting in the way. Should the problem remain you might seek consultation, particularly from someone who is familiar with GAD and CBT, if such a person is available.

This empathic connection will be an essential ingredient for you and your client while you are working together in this structured program. The client needs to know that he has a good emotional relationship with you to count on as you begin the sometimes challenging work of overcoming his GAD. You will serve as teacher, ally, and guide. After all, more than anything else, CBT is a therapy of education leading to new experience. The best learning of new concepts and skills takes place from the foundation of an empathic connection between you and your client. While this skill-based CBT approach is different from other therapies that focus primarily on the exploration of feelings or inner conflicts, your client will gain a great deal as long as he feels solid in his empathic connection with you.

Client Goals

Next, it is important to review with your client his goals for therapy. This usually starts with his wanting to eliminate his anxiety. Make inquiries to find out exactly what this would mean for him. You want to engage him in discussing the specifics of his behaviors that demonstrate anxiety and what he hopes his behaviors will look like when he finishes therapy. Periodically over the course of therapy you will return to his goals to determine what kind of progress he is making and generate additional goals as he moves forward.

In addition to individual goals, clients in general will learn how to manage their anxiety. Once they become aware of triggers that are personally threatening in their lives, they can recognize early warning signs as new threats begin to surface. Rather than escalating to an immediate anxiety attack, as may have been characteristic of a client before, he'll start to feel able to sort through the available choices and make a response that he feels good about. At the same time he'll be practicing skills of physical relaxation that will allow him to release some (perhaps most) of the stress of his day-to-day life. Countering an old tendency to avoid the subjects that make him feel anxious, he'll be better able to take on what is important to him and then see it through to a satisfying conclusion. By anticipating those particular situations that still carry greater anxiety potential for him, he can make sure to provide himself with extra support to minimize the impact. In drawing strength from these cumulative gains in his everyday life, he may eventually feel ready to address some of those fundamental beliefs (referred to as "core beliefs" in this manual) that originated his anxiety cycle in the first place. At that time he will feel sufficiently confident to challenge those archaic rules and revise the beliefs about himself and his world more in keeping with what he values now. This work with beliefs can be quite involved and often continues after the conclusion of therapy. While anxiety doesn't disappear completely, it can be a well-managed facet of a life the client finds to be fulfilling.

In discussing goals for treatment, try to find out if your client has an underlying hope of eliminating anxiety from his life altogether. While this is an understandable wish, it is not feasible and would set the client up for inevitable disappointment with therapy. Obviously, anxiety is a normal reaction, particularly in this stress-ridden culture we've created. While you can help "normalize" some degree of anxiety in a client's life after therapy, his wish to eliminate all anxiety ought to remain an ongoing topic in your work together. It will probably surface from time to time and will provide a good understanding of what happens when he gets disappointed or frustrated with therapy. Once the desire is brought to light he will likely be able to frame a more realistic goal. Over time this might be one of the core beliefs that he chooses to revise in his own way.

Assessment

The assessment phase of the first session usually takes thirty to forty-five minutes. For a diagnosis of GAD, a semistructured interview is used that covers a series of topics, each with several questions. While it is important to address all the topics in the interview, in real life it is impractical and seldom necessary to proceed in a set order. As stated previously, history-taking should proceed in a way that allows the client to tell his story with minimal direction from you. This is a time to listen carefully and build rapport. Thus, the order in which the following seven topics are covered will largely be determined by the client.

History

1. When do you first remember being anxious? What problems or difficulties did it cause for you? Were you anxious as a child? How did you deal with the anxiety at the time? How has anxiety affected your life in general?

2. Has anyone in your family's history had significant anxiety? Are you aware of any therapy or medications they received? How much contact did you have with these individuals? Did their anxiety have an influence upon you?

Current Level of Impairment

3. How does anxiety affect your current life? Do you notice problems or difficulties? Is anxiety a factor in your personal relationships? Does it influence your experience at work or school?

4. Does anxiety affect your patterns of sleep or appetite? Are there changes in your level of energy or fatigue? Do you notice problems with your concentration? Does anxiety cause you to react in any ways that are possibly dangerous or harmful to yourself?

5. Are you currently going through significant changes in your life? What hardships are you dealing with? Is anyone you care about in a bad situation that leads you to feel anxious? Do you worry about natural disasters? Do you worry about being homeless?

Differential Diagnosis

6. Depression: Do you have strong or persistent feelings of depression? Do you feel hopeless or helpless? Do you have thoughts of dying or suicide?

Other Anxiety Disorders

(Question the client in detail if there are any indications of any of these disorders.)

7. Panic attacks: Do you ever have a sudden onset of intense fear?

Agoraphobia: Do you avoid places that would be difficult to escape from?

Phobia: Do you have any strong fears about a specific thing or situation? Do you have intense anxiety in social situations? Do you have any obsessions or compulsions?

PTSD: Do you have a strong recall of a trauma from the past?

Anger

8. Do you lose your temper? Does anxiety cause you to be irritable?

Substance Abuse

9. How much alcohol do you drink in an average week? Do you get drunk? Do you use recreational drugs? What is your pattern of use? Have you had any problems with work or family due to the use of alcohol or drugs? Does anyone think you have an alcohol or drug problem?

Prior Treatment

10. Have you been in treatment for your anxiety? What kind of care did you receive? What were the outcomes? What did you learn that was helpful or useful?

Physical Status and Medications

11. Are you taking any medications prescribed by a physician? Are any of those medications specifically for treatment of your anxiety? Have there been

changes in the dose or your patterns of use? What do you feel are the benefits? Do you notice any problems or side effects? (If your client has been taking a benzodiazepine tranquilizer such as Xanax or Klonopin for a year or more, there may be issues of dependency that can mimic the symptoms of anxiety. You might consider suggesting that your client seek evaluation by a physician regarding this possibility.)

12. Do you have any current physical illnesses? Has a physician raised a concern about your health? (A number of general medical conditions can cause anxiety symptoms, so if general medical problems and anxiety symptoms coexist, refer the client to a physician. Depending upon your client's responses, you might want to inquire regarding:

> endocrine conditions, such as hyper- or hypothyroidism;
> cardiovascular conditions, such as congestive heart failure;
> respiratory conditions, such as chronic obstructive pulmonary disease;
> metabolic conditions, such as vitamin B12 deficiency; and/or
> neurological conditions, such as neoplasms.)

13. Do you experience body tension, sweating, or difficulty breathing? Do you feel restless or on edge? Have you noticed a change in your sex life?

14. Which over-the-counter medications do you use? How much caffeine do you consume? Do you take vitamins or supplements?

Current Resources

15. How have you been coping with your anxiety? What helps you feel as though anxiety has less control of your life? Do you have a sense of confidence when you make headway with your anxiety?

16. How strong is your motivation to overcome your anxiety? Are you willing to spend up to two hours a day doing homework that will help you improve? Do you think you will keep going even if there are times when you feel frustrated, disappointed, or bored?

17. Do the people in your life—partner, family, friends, colleagues at work—understand your anxiety? Do you think they support you in your efforts to overcome it? Do you think anyone might knowingly or unknowingly want you to remain as you are?

18. Do you have the time and financial resources to follow through with treatment to completion—approximately ten to twelve weekly sessions with daily homework assignments between sessions?

Sharing Your Conclusions

Both you and your client have much to gain from the first session's assessment. In addition to its providing a platform for building your alliance with him, it also allows you to learn about the nature of this individual. What are the unique qualities of his anxiety? How do those qualities contribute to a fundamental understanding of him?

The client can also expect to benefit from the assessment. By joining you in examining the elements of his life, he is likely to see new meanings and perspectives in his experience. Explain to your client why you are asking those particular questions and how you go about making sense of his answers, because the better you can walk your client through the process with you, the greater his understanding. This is the beginning of his education about the diagnosis of GAD.

As this collaboration helps demystify the diagnosis, your client has an opportunity to begin seeing a different framework to comprehend those aspects of his experience that may have set him apart from the mainstream. Be aware this can be a strong emotional process for your client. He may experience apprehension at what is being stirred up, relief that someone seems to finally understand what he is experiencing, sorrow at what may have been the unnecessary waste and loss in his life, or hope that he can actually feel better by starting on this process with you. As this emotional dialogue gets underway you want to provide him a therapeutic context in which he feels that you are truly interested in what he says and that you really care about him as a person. If he senses these qualities in the relationship with you, he will likely then feel okay about expressing and exploring his feelings with you. Though it is still only the first session, the therapy between you and your client has already begun.

While a wide range of people can benefit from this protocol treatment for GAD, it is important not to overlook certain limitations of this approach. An individual needs to have a good measure of stability in his feelings and his life circumstances in order to undertake this work (Young 1990). In your initial assessment of your client you will be making the important decision of whether or not he is stable enough to continue. Is he prone to suicidal thoughts or actions? Does he use drugs or alcohol in ways that suggest abuse or dependence? Is he facing a crisis in a primary relationship? Is there serious unrest in his work setting? Are close family members exposed to harm or danger? To the extent that these factors are present, you as the therapist will need to make a determination as to whether or not the individual has the psychological resources to undertake treatment for GAD at this time. If the other problems are sufficiently serious, it will probably make sense to deal with those urgent issues first in a crisis-intervention mode. Not only does the immediate damage of the situation need to stopped, but the GAD is probably made worse by the ongoing crisis.

Fortunately, the decision whether to treat GAD or the crisis as the greater priority does not rest on your shoulders alone. You'll be discussing every step of this process with your client. Starting from the initial assessment you will be inquiring about the various pressures and crises in your client's life. How does his view of these events compare with yours? Share your process of arriving at a diagnosis step by step with your client so he can give input and understand your decision. If you see there would be immediate crises or other issues competing with effective treatment for GAD, convey your thoughts to him in detail. After all, it will ultimately be up to him to decide which (if any) therapy he will undertake, and a clear and solid agreement with you is essential. Perhaps the decision will be to deal with the crisis first, and then begin the GAD protocol afterward. Or, if the crisis is not too overwhelming, the GAD work could begin with regular attention to the side issue until it is resolved. Obviously, either of these alternate paths would require steady and ongoing communication between you and the client.

Treatment Recommendations

During the last ten to fifteen minutes of the first session you will engage with your client in a dialogue about the treatment you are undertaking together. The more complete his understanding of how and what you will be doing in therapy, the better he can ally himself with the process. This begins at the opening of therapy and continues throughout your work. Encourage him to ask questions, as this is how he arrives at a deeper sense of the therapy.

In the process you also communicate that you have a treatment plan by which you will be able to help him. This develops his trust in you and the therapy you will be doing together. It also sets in motion the client's hope that he may actually be able to overcome his anxiety. More likely than not your client comes to you feeling rather hopeless that his efforts to change on his own so far have failed. For him to engage in a collaborative relationship with you he needs to begin to feel some sense of hope that the process of therapy can really help him make gains. In your empathic connection with him as well as your belief in the therapy program, you bring a sense of hope to your client.

Session Summary

The therapy hour can close with a brief summary of the first session. For example, "Our purpose is for you to learn skills for overcoming your GAD. In the process you will gain a greater sense of confidence that you can handle your anxiety on your own. The therapy will take about ten to twelve weeks and you will practice what you learn in daily homework. Research shows that of the people with GAD who complete a therapy program such as this, 70 percent will experience full relief from their GAD. The remaining people report significant improvement in their anxiety. If you make a commitment to the therapy and the homework, I think you can make strong progress."

Feedback from Client

After summarizing the session, it's important to ask the client if he has any questions and allow yourself adequate time to answer them.

Homework for This Session

1. Ask the client to read session one of the Client Manual. This will help him understand the nature of his problem and the first stages of treatment.

2. You will also ask him to fill out the State Trait Anxiety Inventory (STAI). (Three blank copies are at the back of his manual.) This provides a baseline for the beginning of treatment and permits comparison with his scores at the midpoint and conclusion of therapy.

Scheduling Worry Time

Monitoring of Current Status

Each new session should begin with your asking the client whether any significant concerns have arisen since the previous session—either related to therapy or otherwise. Before proceeding to agenda setting, the client needs the opportunity to express these concerns and feel resolved about moving on. If a personal crisis has occurred, some or even all of the session may need to focus on dealing with the client's feelings before you and she return to the treatment protocol. A major event such as the loss of a job or diagnosis of a serious illness usually means that behavioral goals will be set aside for a few weeks. Your empathic response to these major life changes is more important than treating GAD.

You'll then want to address any pressing issues in her life that are related to her anxiety. Together you should aim for your client to feel more stable and less vulnerable to immediate anxiety. Unless there is a major life crisis, this early discussion should not take more than ten minutes in order to allow full time for the new skills you will be covering—try not to let the new skills get pushed aside by other conversation. Managing the session for adequate time to teach new skills communicates to the client that these skills are important and sets the client's expectation that in each future session there will be a therapeutic skill to be learned in addition to the mutual discussion about clinical issues.

Agenda Setting

As you and your client are developing the agenda for this session, pay attention to how she describes the worries in her life. Are they always seen as negative? Does she ever offer ways that her anxieties lead to good outcomes? During this session you and she will focus on worry topics that may lead to positive results. The more you can incorporate her natural anxiety topics into the therapy work the better the learning experience.

Specific goals for this session include:

1. Reviewing the client's homework from session 1

2. Educating her about worry and the skill of scheduling worry time

3. Guiding her through a five-minute worrry-time exercise

4. Introducing her to the benefits of starting a Daily Worry Record

5. Exploring the correlations between the client's personal relationships and worry

Review of Homework from Session 1

What reactions did your client experience upon reading session 1 in her manual? Is she beginning to feel comfortable with this discussion of anxiety and therapy? Encourage any questions, comments, agreements, and (especially) disagreements. You want to encourage your client's independent reading and thinking about this material rather than leading her to believe she is to automatically conform to what is written whether she believes it or not.

You will interpret the results of your client's STAI during this session using the instructions and norm tables that appear in appendix 1 of this manual. Read over her responses. Were there any that stood out to you (high or low) in contrast to how you would have expected the client to respond based upon the first session and the diagnostic interview? Discuss these outliers as an opportunity to learn more about your client and to refine your clinical formulation of the case.

How does the client feel about her STAI scores as they compare to the general population? Does this fit with what she expected, or is it something different? What kind of anxiety scores would your client like to have by the end of her therapy? What goals do you foresee? Can you and your client identify individual items that are particular targets for change?

Concepts and Skills

Psychoeducation

Worry

A cognitive-behavioral view of GAD begins with the premise that not all worry is bad. A therapeutic approach that implied that worry is somehow completely wrong would be guilty of black-and-white thinking. CBT regards such black-and-white thinking as an all-too-common cognitive distortion of the complexities of true experience. After all, real life usually comes in full color, right? So the first thing you want to avoid doing with your clients is painting worry with a black brush.

To this end your client's first new skill is scheduling worry time. This is a simple procedure: you ask your client to select a worthwhile topic associated with her worry and commit some time to it. The theoretical premise behind this is that the client will learn that there can be value in focusing her anxious energies. There can also be a paradoxical benefit in that the client's skill in determining when to worry can translate to a new ability to determine when it is *not* necessary to worry.

One of the reasons that scheduling worry time is the first skill you ask your client to learn with you is because it is a relatively straightforward task. Review the following material in advance of the session and be prepared to guide your client in a trial during her session. The worry time should be no longer than five minutes, probably less. Help her really get into the experience of worrying. She should make her statements out loud to you and you should reflect back similar thoughts echoing her anxiety. Make the worry experience as thorough as possible. Don't be surprised if you find that there is some shared amusement during the process, as you and your client join forces in what might be characterized as a "neurotic duet."

Skill Building

Scheduling Worry Time

1. **Pick a Worthwhile Topic to Worry About**
   There can be many random little subjects that we may worry about, but they don't amount to much. Ask your client to try to identify a topic that is worthwhile to spend some time with. It may involve a big decision she needs to make. Or it may be her preparation for an important performance in school, work, or athletics. The topic should have some type of meaningful result in her day-to-day life.

2. **Set Aside Five Minutes**
   Let the client know that the worry time she'll be practicing in this session with you will take five minutes. Keep track of the time so your client doesn't need to focus on it. Outside of her sessions, she will take time that does not require a strong mental focus elsewhere. She may use time during her commute, a coffee break, or a shower. She should make sure it has some kind of natural ending to it because she doesn't want the worrying to go on indefinitely.

3. **Focus on the Topic at Hand**
   Remind your client to try not to let her attention drift in and out. She needs the benefit that comes from her mind having concentrated its focus on the issue that is bothering her. And when the worry time is finished she needs the mental relief of disengaging from what has been her full concentration. To this end, have your client state her worry thoughts out loud to you. This will help keep her focused. Explain that the benefit comes when her mind is concentrated on the topic that is bothering her. You can reflect back to her empathic comments that reflect the anxiety of the topic. For example, if she says, "I'm worried about not finishing a job at work," you could reflect, "You feel a lot of pressure to perform." Your remarks keep the flow going and let your client know that you are emotionally connected to her.

4. **Don't Dwell on the Topic When You've Finished with Worry Time**
   When you finish this exercise in session, talk with your client about how she feels, rather than getting back into the topic itself. This will model to her how to leave the topic behind. When your client practices this at home, she needs to let go of the topic after the exercise and move into her time-off from worrying. She should try not to let the anxieties leak in when she would prefer to be doing something else with her life. Demonstrate for her how she can turn loose of the

topic go while reminding herself that there is another worry time scheduled later. It's not a perfect solution, but it can help reduce some of the anxiety.

The Daily Worry Record

In this session you will teach your client how to complete a Daily Worry Record. This is really quite simple: you will ask your client to make her own assessment of her worry. Each day—using a scale from 0 to 100, with 0 being no anxiety at all and 100 being the single worst anxiety she has ever experienced—she'll rate her average level of anxiety through the day and her level of peak anxiety. There is a blank Daily Worry Record in the second chapter of your client's manual and for each week of treatment thereafter. (Following is an example of the form your client will fill out this week.)

Daily Worry Record: Week One

Date	Average Level of Anxiety	Peak Level of Anxiety

Remind your client that it's best to make this determination in the evening so she can review the events of the entire day. She should make every effort to do this each day and not let the assessments stack up until later, because that makes it difficult to remember and reconstruct the events of a given day. Let her know that you hope the Daily Worry Record will become a habit for her throughout the course of her therapy.

Naturally you'll respond to any questions that arise. Occasionally clients will not understand the premise of the Daily Worry Record. You can help them recognize that for there to be changes in their anxiety there must first be a good sense of exactly what levels exist. Compare the procedure to a medical doctor who keeps a daily record of a patient's temperature to chart the course of a fever. Be aware that there may be more variations in day-to-day assessments of anxiety than clients initially expected. Tell your clients that this is a good sign because it shows that the anxiety is not as monolithic and intractable as they first thought.

Make sure to follow up on the Daily Worry Record at the beginning of each new session. Not only does this demonstrate that you consider the activity to be worthwhile, but it offers a good overview of the week and helps establish those issues that should be addressed in the new session.

Beginning with the next session, you'll also want to follow up on the client's "Therapy Journal" an important and personal document the client will develop over the course of therapy. Per the instructions in her Client Manual, she will purchase a simple spiral notebook and use it for therapy only. (You may want to remind her at the end of this session to do so.) She will write each day about her experiences with the skill she is learning. This will allow her to reflect upon these new events and what they mean to her. What feelings does she notice? Are there alternate thoughts she becomes aware of? What, if any, experiences were easier than she expected? What did she think of her results? How can she modify the processes next time to have better outcomes? Make sure the client brings her Therapy Journal with her to the sessions, because it will be a fine source for you to learn more about her week and it will provide for you fresh accounts of topics that warrant further discussion.

Personal Relationships and Scheduling Worry Time

Each session in this manual will explore the connections between the new skill presented during the session and the client's ongoing personal relationships. GAD's impact on your clients' personal relationships is one of the most important aspects of the ongoing therapy between you and your clients. Your face-to-face contact with the client brings to life these vital interpersonal issues in a way that workbook study alone cannot. To that end, I encourage you to ask your client the questions that will appear under the heading "Personal Relationships and . . ." in each session.

When the client selects a topic to worry about, does it include her contact with other people? Can it be resolved by working through the anxiety on the client's own, or does it reveal some underlying problem in the relationship that calls for more attention? Which people, past or present, have influenced the way in which the client regards her anxiety? Scheduling worry time usually occurs for the client by herself. Does this feel satisfactory to her or is she more accustomed to worrying in the company of someone else? Does she feel better or worse when worrying alone versus being with somebody?

Session Summary

Briefly summarize the material covered in the session. Try to reflect those learning points personally notable to your client. If your client disagrees with or seems to not understand your summary, you should ask her questions to find out why.

Feedback from Client

At the conclusion of each session, ask your client for feedback about the usefulness of the material and any questions that may remain. Encourage her to give feedback so that you can address any concerns that may have arisen.

Homework for This Session

1. After the client has practiced worry time once or twice during the first session, you will suggest that she do it at least once a day between now and the next session. She should make note of her experiences in her Therapy Journal.

2. The client will also complete her first Daily Worry Record this week. Remind her to bring it with her the next time you meet.

3. Prior to the next session your client should complete the "preview to session three" that appears in her manual. Each preview in her manual contains a brief statement of the problem covered in the session to come as well as a description of the solution she will learn from you. She will also be asked to complete a ten-question self-assessment to see what difficulties and strengths she has in these areas. Hopefully, the previews will prepare her for a discussion of the topic and she will arrive to her session prepared with some issues to discuss.

Relaxation

Monitoring of Current Status

As described in the last session, you should begin by asking the client whether any significant concerns—related to therapy or otherwise—have arisen since the previous session. Remember to try to keep this early discussion under ten minutes. (You may want to review "Monitoring of Current Status" in session 2.)

Starting with this session, you should initiate a custom with your client in which you and he discuss his Worry Record at the beginning of each session. This is a convenient way of getting a sense of the client's current level of anxiety. Note the number of anxiety experiences described. How does this compare with what you expected based upon your clinical evaluation of the first two sessions? You may want to comment if the contrast is striking. What trends do you notice about the high anxiety experiences of the week? Perhaps certain automatic thoughts come up over and over, or perhaps there are particular type of events that seem to trigger the anxiety. Ask your client what patterns he was aware of at the time. Share your ideas in an open-ended manner and suggest that your client see if they fit with his experience. Did he observe any change in his level of anxiety as a result of completing the Worry Record? He may notice that he felt better sooner or, perhaps, he might be aware that he felt worse longer. Obviously these would be ideal topics to explore in therapy. Were there any occasions of anxiety that he did not enter in the Worry Record? If so, can you discern an underlying reason or impediment? These would be crucial areas to discuss as they may signal some reluctance or difficulty on the part of the client that needs to be addressed with you.

Agenda Setting

You and your client will go over the ten-question self-assessment that he completed from the preview section of his manual. Are there any questions that really stood out to him? How do these add to what you and he have discussed so far in therapy? The odd-numbered items reflect the variety of ways that anxiety can express itself—ask your client which ones were especially strong for him, and keep these in mind during your session together. Also, ask your client if he is aware of where he experiences the anxiety in his body. Does he notice any anxious feelings or thoughts in particular that are related to this week's self-assessment?

The even-numbered items reflect various ways of managing anxiety so that it does not take control. What areas of strength are shown in your client's responses? At the beginning of each session, ask him if he notices areas of growth for himself since the beginning of therapy. Discuss with him what areas of change he wants to make that could reduce the problems of anxiety as well as increase his coping skills. Ask him if these fit with his initial goals for therapy—you may decide together to add new areas to his therapy. You might want to revisit this self-assessment in a week and a month to see if there have been any changes by that time.

You'll also want to ask what your client would like to share from the writing in his Therapy Journal. By checking in each session you show that you think the journal is important. The client learns to make note of questions to be posed to you in the next session, such as surprising results from the homework or indications of a broader awareness of his anxiety. Suggest that the client read his journal prior to sharing it with you. You might anticipate the client's discomfort and/or self-criticism that can be eased by your explaining, "You can learn about yourself by reading your own journal. Try not to be too hard on yourself. This journal is a free expression of feelings and ideas, not a perfect document." The client's reaction to his Therapy Journal will be significantly influenced by the attitude toward it that you demonstrate to him.

Specific goals for this session include:

1. Reviewing homework from session 2

2. Introducing your client to a relaxation technique called progressive muscle relaxation (PMR)

3. Exploring correlations between the client's personal relationships and relaxation.

Review of Homework from Session 2

Make sure you follow up on homework each and every time it is undertaken. Ask whether the client has practiced worry time daily, as you had suggested. What did your client learn from these experiences? What was surprising and did not turn out as expected? Suggest that the client read to you some of his experiences with worry time as recorded in his Therapy Journal. This gives you a firsthand sense of what he is writing about outside of the session.

Were there any days when he did not practice worry time? If so, what seemed to get in the way? Perhaps it was fatigue, excessive worry about a particular topic, or discouragement about whether the method would really work. Whatever the case may be, you want to encourage and facilitate his identifying the factors that are involved. The more he can identify these kinds of obstacles, the better you and he can plan future homework that he *can* successfully complete.

Concepts and Skills

Psychoeducation

Relaxation

The more that a client can create for himself the physical experience of relaxation, the less he will feel anxiety—at least during that moment. While this is not an ultimate or exclusive answer to anxiety, it is a good place to begin. Your goal is to show your client that there's an alternative to his body's habit of feeling stress and tension. This is a physical intervention that provides a platform for the emotional and mental changes to come. Time spent developing skills for relaxation will pay off in the client's openness and willingness to accept other interventions later.

Do you feel comfortable guiding your client in physical relaxation? Has this been part of your background and training? Do you practice relaxation or meditation in your personal life? If all your answers are not strongly affirmative, don't feel intimidated—relaxation is a straightforward skill for you to learn. Go through the daily practice of progressive muscle relaxation (PMR) as you will be asking your client to do. You'll gain personal experience as to whether this technique really works, you'll be able to anticipate the kinds of questions or issues your clients might have, and you'll develop your own sense of authority. Do the complete four-week cycle as outlined in the Client Manual. You may also be interested in additional books, tapes, and workshops that focus on relaxation (three excellent tapes are listed in the back of this manual, under "Suggested Reading").

You may expect that at least some of your clients will try to take shortcuts in their PMR practice. We live in a high-speed culture and people who are anxious are often the speediest of all. You should remain constant in recommending the twice-daily practice to your clients, since this has proven to help the greatest number of people over the long run. If your client insists on cutting back, suggest that it be done as an "experiment" to assess his results compared to a standard approach. Modifications can then be made as necessary. Either way, keep the lines of communication open and avoid a power struggle. Most importantly, don't fail to ask about relaxation each and every session, even if you anticipate your client's answer to be negative. Your polite inquiry shows that you consider relaxation to be an important part of recovery from anxiety.

Finally, be aware of the aspects of your client's body that seem naturally relaxed. By your pointing out these areas of physical comfort from time to time, he can begin to identify what the practice of relaxation will ultimately feel like when he is finished with therapy. This can provide your client with a sense of initial encouragement, and it also counteracts a tendency in this early part of therapy for your client to feel that he is completely messed up and has to learn everything all over. If this attitude is not resolved, it can snowball to one of the main reasons why he might drop out of treatment. Starting with those times and places that he already feels relaxed helps validate that he knows more about this process than he thinks he does.

Skill Building
Progressive Muscle Relaxation

This relaxation sequence will require approximately four weeks of daily practice. Your client will start with twice-a-day exercises for the first two weeks. Ask him to think of this as a concentrated dose to educate his body to the benefits of relaxation. Most people find these experiences pleasurable as long as they set aside sufficient time for practice. He will be using a method called progressive muscle relaxation, or PMR. The first week involves exercises for sixteen muscle groups; the entire exercise requires approximately one half hour to complete. As he experiences greater skill at relaxation, he can modify the PMR exercises in the second week for eight muscle groups. He should continue with the twice-daily routine.

During weeks three and four he ought to try to engage in relaxation exercises at least once a day. During this time he will learn a shorthand version of PMR as well as what is called "cue-controlled relaxation," which he can use in his day-to-day life whenever anxious feelings arise. He should continue to devote daily time to relaxation from the fourth week onward.

Guiding Your Client through PMR. In this session you will guide your client through his first experience of progressive muscle relaxation. Even if he has had other relaxation experiences, it is nonetheless a good idea for him to go through these steps with you. PMR is unusually well suited to deal with anxiety compared to other relaxation methods he may have learned. Once he knows PMR, he can determine which approach works best for him.

The initial PMR process will take approximately one half hour, but you can obviously adjust it to make the process as comfortable as possible for your client. This starts with your own familiarity with the method and includes sufficient rapport between you and the client for him to be able to really relax under your guidance.

Have your client take a comfortable seat in your office. His head and arms need to be physically supported. Ask if he feels okay about shutting his eyes during the process. If he would rather not, suggest that he fix his gaze on a neutral object or look out the window. It's time to begin.

Arms

1. Clasp both hands into fists and roll your wrists with knuckles pointing upward. Hold the tightness for ten seconds and pay attention to the tension in your muscles. Now let go of the tightness and let your arms relax onto the chair. Notice the change in sensation. Repeat by making fists again for ten seconds and then relaxing for twenty seconds.

2. Next, bend both elbows and flex your biceps. Hold this "bodybuilder" pose for ten seconds, then let go of the tension. Your arms feel heavy and warm. Flex a second time, then relax.

3. Lock your elbows straight and stretch your arms toward the floor. Feel the tension up and down your arms. Release after ten seconds and relax for twenty seconds. Repeat.

Legs

1. Flex your toes by drawing them toward your head while you tighten your shin and calf muscles. Hold, then release by letting your feet hang loosely. Repeat.

2. Tighten your lower leg while pointing your toes. Hold the position, then release as you return your toes to a natural position. Repeat.

3. Tense your inner thigh muscles by pressing your knees together as hard as you can. Release, and feel the sense of ease spread throughout your legs. Repeat.

4. Tighten your buttocks and thighs. Increase the tension by straightening your legs and pushing down hard through your heels. Hold the position, then let go. Repeat.

Midsection

1. Gently arch your back. Hold the tension, then relax so your back is flat against the back of the chair. Repeat.

2. Take a deep breath and fill your lungs. Contract all the muscles in your chest and abdomen. Hold, then exhale and release all the air. Repeat.

3. Stretch your shoulders backward, as though you were trying to touch your shoulder blades together. Hold the position, then let your arms drop by your sides. Repeat.

4. Raise your shoulders as high as you can, as though you are trying to touch your ears. Hold, then let your shoulders drop as though to the floor. Repeat.

Head

1. Tilt your head backward and extend your chin toward the ceiling. Hold, then release and bring your chin to rest on your chest. Repeat.

2. Clench your jaw and push your tongue up to the roof of your mouth. Hold, then release to feel the relaxation of your lips. Repeat.

3. Close your eyes tightly and smile, stretching your mouth as wide open as you can. Hold it, then relax. Repeat.

4. Raise your eyebrows as high as you can and feel the tension across the top of your head. Hold, and relax. Repeat.

Personal Relationships and Relaxation

Is there anyone with whom your client feels relaxed? In whose presence does he experience some degree of pleasure? With inquiry during the session, try to see if there are any relationships that are an exception to the client's experience of wall-to-wall anxiety. Perhaps this may be an opening to recognize the kinds of personal contacts that support his recovery from anxiety. These would be people the client would likely seek out for more contact. Perhaps you and your client can figure out what about these relationships helps reduce his anxiety and determine whether those qualities can be applied more broadly.

At the same time the client will also be exploring the question of which kinds of personal contacts cause him to have strong negative experiences of physical tension. What is it about these relationships that seem to cause his body to sound the stress alarm? Do these same individuals in their personal lives show a tendency toward physical relaxation or physical tension? Sometimes it seems as if such body tensions between two people can mirror each other, although neither individual is necessarily aware of it. These collected observations can be helpful to the client in better understanding the origins of his anxiety as well as choosing the kinds of close connections with people that favor his continued progress.

Session Summary

Briefly summarize the material covered in the session. Try to reflect those learning points personally notable to your client. If your client disagrees with or seems to not understand your summary, you should ask him questions to find out why.

Feedback from Client

At the conclusion of each session, ask your client for feedback about the usefulness of the material and any questions that may remain. Encourage him to give feedback so that you can address any concerns that may have arisen.

Homework for This Session

1. Ask your client to practice relaxation on a twice-daily basis for the next two weeks and once daily for two weeks after that. Hopefully, he had a positive initial experience of PMR in today's session with you, but be aware of any reservations the client may voice. If the schedule feels overwhelming to him, suggest that he use a "one day at a time" approach. It may also prove helpful if you problem-solve with him how he could clear enough time in his daily life to do the PMR. If he happens to fall short of doing some of his practice, try to make sure he resumes at the next opportunity. You want him to feel sufficient hope for future gains that he not quit altogether.

2. He should continue writing in his Therapy Journal. Ask him to address his emotional experiences as well as physical awarenesses that occur during relaxation practice. For example, does he discover the parts of his body most likely to hold daily stress? What is the easiest area to relax? The most difficult? Does the client write differently following a PMR session when he is more relaxed? Do his emotions feel different to him when he is relaxed compared with when he is stressed? Suggest that the client also write about general issues of anxiety that come up during the week. He may choose to discuss some of this material when he brings his Therapy Journal to the next session.

3. Remind him to complete his Daily Worry Record and bring it with him to the next session.

4. Remind him to read the "Preview to Session 4" that appears in his manual. As discussed in the previous session, he will need to complete the ten-question self-assessment that appears in that section of his manual and bring it with him to the next session with you.

Session 4

Risk Assessment

Monitoring of Current Status

Again, begin by asking the client whether any significant concerns—related to therapy or otherwise—have arisen since the previous session. Remember to try to keep this early discussion under ten minutes. (You may want to review "Monitoring of Current Status" in session 2.)

As described in the last session, you and your client will discuss the Worry Record that she kept over the course of the last week so that you can get a sense of her current level of anxiety. (For more details on examining the record, review "monitoring of current Status," in session 3.)

Agenda Setting

You and your client will go over the ten-question self-assessment that she completed from the preview section of her manual. You will also ask her what she would like to share from the writing in her Therapy Journal. (For more information on examining the self-assessment and the Therapy Journal, review "Agenda Setting" in session 3.)

Because anxiety is driven by a perception of threat, you and your client in this session will begin to assess the kinds of threats she experiences. This process of risk assessment will give her a greater sense of clarity as to the origins of her anxiety. When you and she are setting the agenda for this session, pay close attention to the types of risk she spontaneously reports because these will be timely subjects for her when she practices risk assessment. In each subsequent session your check-in will include her report of situations in which her experience of risk remains high.

Specific goals for this session include:

1. Reviewing homework from session 3

2. Educating the client about risk assessment and guiding her through her first in-session risk assessment

3. Educating her about creating a weekly Thought Record

4. Exploring correlations between her personal relationships and risk assessment

Review of Homework from Session 3

Hopefully your client was able to experience some positive results from the twice-daily relaxation this week. Careful questioning can help your client put into words some of her initial favorable experiences—for example, "Did you notice that any areas of your body felt more at ease after you finished the relaxation?" and "Were you aware of any positive feelings during relaxation?" In the early stages she probably will not have full awareness of what is happening in her body during relaxation. Reviewing homework together with her can help her develop greater capacity to notice the physical changes that are taking place. This emerging skill of awareness will, in turn, assist your client in the relaxation she will practice in the weeks to come.

Was she able to keep herself on a schedule of twice-daily relaxation? If she fell short, did she resume at the next opportunity? Doing so is recognized as quite valuable to therapy because it means that even with brief interruptions in homework, your client is learning to keep on track for longer-term gains. If she was able to do only a bit or was unable to do any of the relaxation, it is crucial to understand exactly why. Don't settle for externalized reasons such as "I was busy," or "I didn't have privacy." These factors are true for practically anyone, but most people manage to do the homework anyway, while some do not. Try to uncover the real underlying reasons, which are usually reflected in negative thoughts such as, "I feel stupid doing this," or "I'd get bored too easily," or "I'm worried I would fail," or "I don't think it will do any good." As these explanations come to light, you and your client can explore the validity of such beliefs as well as the consequences of letting them squelch relaxation before it even gets started. Suggest that your client try just enough relaxation to determine whether the negative beliefs are really true—or whether there are truly greater gains to be realized.

Concepts and Skills

Psychoeducation

Risk Assessment

Your client likely senses that most everything around her is dangerous. This might include threats to any of the following: her personal safety, her important relationships, her financial security, or even her ability to feel good about herself. Your goal in this session is to bring her process of assessing risk out into the open. After all, the client is probably not entirely aware of all the judgments she is making. The judgments often come so fast and are so automatic that the individual has little objective sense of what is really happening to her. In therapy you are slowing down the process so that she can study it step by step. That alone initiates change. The client begins to see where she may overrespond to current situations on the basis of damage done by old threats. She can begin to recognize that there can be a variety of ways of seeing a situation and she's not obliged to always assume as true the most frightening view. Finally, she can reaffirm to herself that there are indeed genuine dangers out there, and she has not necessarily been overreacting to everything in her life.

Hopefully, during the preceding sessions, you've been paying attention to what situations seem to feel safe to your client and which appear dangerous. When you describe to her how risk assessment works, it helps to have practical examples from her recent experiences that bring this skill to life. The hardest part for her may be coming up with Worst Possible Outcomes. Sometimes this discussion itself feels threatening to a client and she may prefer to avoid it. Or perhaps the prospects seem outlandish to your client and she resists putting herself in a situation that she thinks makes her look silly. Gently persist. You can help by providing some samples of what Worst Outcomes might be and explaining them in a sensible manner so your client doesn't feel foolish. The more personal you can make the Worst Outcomes the better. This is a skill that develops over time.

Practice several versions of risk assessment during the session. Use real-life experiences from the client's day-to-day life. If she draws a blank, you can provide examples you've observed in her experience derived from your therapy work so far. It would be rather unusual if at the conclusion of each risk assessment when she re-rated anxiety, it had always managed to disappear. If this happens to be what your client is reporting, it may be because this is what she thinks she's supposed to say to you. You can reinforce the obvious fact that serious anxiety doesn't simply vanish just because we undertake a risk assessment. This can help her accept her initial progress resulting from these new therapy skills, while acknowledging her full recovery probably requires a longer path.

Skill Building

Assessing Risk Step by Step

With a week's practice your client should possess good skills in risk assessment. This will permit her to study a situation that seems threatening and become aware of her reactions (and whether or not she is anxious). The stage is then set for her to make a response that deals with the threat. You will want to communicate this sense of confidence in her as you teach your client this new skill. While it would be impossible for her to control all future situations to keep anxiety from arising, with a solid ability to assess risk she can achieve a feeling that she can deal with just about anything that comes up. If, in the early stages, she is unsure of how to perform a given step of the risk assessment, gently guide her to her best tentative answer and keep moving ahead. As long as she doesn't get bogged down in the process, the overall outcome is more important than individual responses along the way. Following are the eight steps you will use in guiding her through the in-session practice.

1. **Name the Triggering Situation**
   This is where you ask your client to think like a detective. She's trying to figure out exactly which triggering situation caused an upturn in her anxiety. Who was she with? What did she say and do? If it's not clear to her immediately, tell her it will probably be a relatively small event. She should use her detective skills to be as specific as possible. Those will be her clues for solving the case.

2. **Rate the Anxiety**
   Tell her to think of the worst anxiety she's ever had: that would be 100. At the other end of the scale, her most relaxed and comfortable time would be 0. She should go with her first impression for where she thinks today's anxiety ranks.

Pretty soon she'll be able to easily tell the difference in her levels of anxiety, say between a 60 and a 40, based upon how each one feels to her.

3. **Describe Other Emotions**

This can be a tricky step. We're paying lots of attention to anxiety, but there may be other emotions that are bothering her, too. Try to figure out what these feelings are. It may help her to think about how she is feeling toward the other people in the triggering situation. She should rank this emotion 0 to 100. It's fine if no other feelings come to the surface right now, but as she works her way through this process she may notice other feelings that come later. Tell her to write them down then.

4. **State the Automatic Thoughts**

The automatic thought is usually the first thing that pops into her head. Most often it's a statement about herself, about her world, or about her future. An automatic thought tends to travel really quickly, but when she catches up with it she often recognizes she's been having that same thought over and over, maybe even for years. In therapy we naturally focus on the thoughts that cause us pain or suffering, but there are plenty of positive automatic thoughts, too.

5. **Imagine the Worst Outcome**

Ask her to think of the worst possible thing that could happen as this situation unfolds. She shouldn't hold herself back. Her anxious mind most likely has already figured out the worst thing that could go wrong, and now she needs to get a good handle on what that is. This is her view of a catastrophic future. Get a full picture. The more realistically she brings the catastrophic future to mind, the better she'll make use of this risk assessment.

6. **Prediction When She's Feeling Anxious**

When she's in a state of high anxiety, the worst outcome seems almost inevitable. After all, anxiety makes her believe more in the catastrophic future, and then it is the fixed idea of catastrophe that makes her more and more anxious. This is how anxiety gets out of control.

7. **Prediction When She's Feeling Stronger**

This calls for some mental juggling. Can she look at her triggering situation without letting anxiety take control? Ask her to imagine she is feeling stronger and she is in a more realistic frame of mind. Don't pressure her to make these changes happen all of a sudden—that takes time. For today, simply ask her to think how the situation may look different to her when she is less anxious. While she's in this mind-set, ask her again about the worst outcome and see how likely it feels to her.

8. **Rerate the Feelings and Thoughts**

At the conclusion of the risk assessment, ask her to rerate her thoughts and feelings using the same 0–100 scale. No one expects huge changes on the basis of this technique alone, but she may notice some relief.

Your Client's Thought Record

Now that you and your client have developed a risk assessment together, she is ready to learn one of the most widely used CBT methods, the "Thought Record." The

Thought Record permits a client to make a clear representation of her mind's experience at a given moment in time. It's quite valuable as a tool of awareness and has been used in CBT since its origins with Dr. Aaron Beck, who pursued a favorite line of questioning with clients: "What is going through your mind right now?" (See Suggested Readings.) So what is going through your client's mind? The Thought Record allows her (and you) to see exactly what comes to the surface in her thoughts and feelings on a moment-by-moment basis.

Ask your client to turn the blank Thought Record in her Client Manual (session 3). Starting in the left-hand column, she will enter the triggering situation from her risk assessment. Next, moving toward the right, she'll record her anxiety and other feelings, including ratings from 0 to 100. Then she'll write down the automatic thoughts that occurred in immediate response to the triggering situation. Ask her to rate—from 0 to 100—to what degree she believed the thought at the moment it occurred. In the next column she will record the very worst outcome that she imagined to the triggering situation. This is a particular modification of the Thought Record for working with issues of anxiety. It seeks to draw full attention to how the imagined worst outcome can make the anxiety cycle worse. The final column on the right-hand side asks the client to rerate her feelings and thoughts, now that she's completed this process.

Note that the steps in the risk assessment of "Predicting outcome when you're feeling anxious" and "Predicting outcome when you're feeling stronger" are not included in the formal Thought Record. It will be obvious, though, to you and your client how these issues relate to the Thought Record your client completes on her own and what you and she will discuss in clinical follow-up.

Completion of a Thought Record will be part of your client's homework this week. This will provide her a much clearer grasp of what is being activated for her in the exact moment that anxiety occurs. She will likely feel less confused or upset by the experience as she gains a fuller understanding of what is happening to her in terms of her own reactions. This also sets in motion her process of determining how she chooses to respond to the situation at hand. Often, by achieving some perspective and distance on the immediate problem, possible solutions begin to appear. The Thought Record can become a reliable first step in that sequence.

The client's Thought Records also provide a wonderful source for you to see how her experiences unfold for her through her own eyes. There is a real vitality to sharing the contents of a Thought Record that was written in the midst of a challenging situation compared to a discussion of the same event in session a week later. Both you and your client will likely be aware of fresh material coming from the Thought Record that brings the clinical experience more to life. There are all kinds of nuances and details and contradictions that make for a rich clinical exchange between you and your client. You can explain these principles to your client as part of your teaching of the Thought Record, but it will not be until you and she share the actual experience of opening one of these up during session that she will really know what you mean.

From this point forward each chapter of your client's guide to treatment will include a blank form that combines the Thought Record with the Daily Worry Record. Through her homework assignments, she is encouraged to fill these out on a regular basis and bring her completed work to the therapy sessions. Obviously you further reinforce the strength of your recommendation when you make a habit of reviewing the Thought Records and Daily Worry Records every week. Clients are given permission to photocopy the blank forms if they need more room in which to work. (Following is an example of the form your client will fill out this week.)

Thought Record

Triggering Situation	Anxiety and Other Feelings	Automatic Thoughts	Worst Outcome	Rerate Feelings and Thoughts

Daily Worry Record: Week Three

Date	Average Level of Anxiety	Peak Level of Anxiety
_____	_____	_____
_____	_____	_____
_____	_____	_____
_____	_____	_____
_____	_____	_____
_____	_____	_____
_____	_____	_____
_____	_____	_____
_____	_____	_____
_____	_____	_____
_____	_____	_____
_____	_____	_____
_____	_____	_____
_____	_____	_____
_____	_____	_____
_____	_____	_____
_____	_____	_____
_____	_____	_____
_____	_____	_____

Personal Relationships and Risk Assessment

Your client is likely to see her world as a relatively unsafe place. After all, this is a big component in the origin of her anxiety. In terms of her personal relationships, she is likewise prone to see herself as small or ineffectual while others are assumed to be large and strong. Explore with your client these deeper feelings about her vulnerability. You can probably find roots in her early experience that continue to the present day. Recognizing her own sense of feeling weak can make the process of learning risk assessment even more essential. Through the use of that skill she can openly examine what makes her feel unsafe and determine whether in fact she has personal resources she was initially overlooking.

Risk assessment relating to other people can also reveal patterns in the client's relationships that reinforce her anxiety. Does she gravitate to people who are truly unsafe and unpredictable, giving her an ongoing sense of danger? Does she prefer the company of people who seem strong (in contrast to her "weakness"), but who undercut her sense of autonomy by their overprotectiveness? Does she avoid relationships with people who would prefer to see her as their equal, rather than falling into the old pattern of mutually acting out the strong/weak split? Do any of these issues arise in the therapeutic relationship between you and the client? Over the course of therapy there will be many opportunities to explore risk assessment in personal relationships.

Session Summary

Briefly summarize the material covered in the session. Try to reflect those learning points personally notable to your client. If your client disagrees with or seems to not understand your summary, you should ask her questions to find out why.

Feedback from Client

At the conclusion of each session, ask your client for feedback about the usefulness of the material and any questions that may remain. Encourage her to give feedback so that you can address any concerns that may have arisen.

Homework for This Session

1. Suggest that your client do at least one risk assessment per day between now and the next session. She should write about her experiences in her Therapy Journal. Remind her that it is optimal to undertake the risk assessment *as the triggering situation* occurs, because in the process of writing the client often figures out her best response to the threat. If it is not feasible to do the writing during the situation itself, the client should wait no longer than that same evening to write it up. Otherwise, the experience goes cold fairly quickly and there is less value in exploring it. The write-up need not take long—five or ten minutes for something straightforward, longer if there is more to explore. Your client

may think there is not enough risk in her life to do a risk assessment for the next seven days. You may remind her that most risks are small and easy to overlook. A good cue is the presence of any anxiety on her part, which probably signals there is some type of risk that is being sensed. Encourage her to do some detective work and figure out what it might be.

2. Your client is now in her second week of self-guided relaxation practice. This week she will learn a modified approach, called PMR-8, that uses just eight muscle groups. Instructions for a self-guided relaxation session are included in her manual (session 4).

3. Suggest to your client that she complete a Thought Record at times during the week that she experiences strong anxiety—certainly at levels of 50 or greater on a scale of 100.

4. Remind her to complete her Daily Worry Record and bring it with her to the next session.

5. Remind her to read the "Preview to Session 5" that appears in her manual. As discussed in session 2, she will need to complete the ten-question self-assessment that appears in that section of her manual and bring it with her to the next session with you.

Session 5

Problem Solving

Monitoring of Current Status

Again, begin by asking the client whether any significant concerns—related to therapy or otherwise—have arisen since the previous session. Remember to try to keep this early discussion under ten minutes. (You may want to review "Monitoring of Current Status" in session 2.)

You and your client will discuss the Worry Record that he kept over the course of the last week so that you can get a sense of his current level of anxiety. (For more details on examining this document, review "Monitoring of Current Status," in session 3.)

This is the first week your client completed a Thought Record along with a Worry Record. In the therapy so far have you noticed that the Worry Records have provided a good overall map of how his anxiety has been on a week-to-week basis? The Thought Record now allows your client to zoom in on specific anxiety situations and make a more detailed account. It is as though the Worry Record provides an overview of several hundred miles of terrain and the Thought Record shows a street-by-street map of an immediate neighborhood. By your linking these two methods in discussion of his current status, you are reinforcing for your client how these records provide a clear understanding of his anxiety as well as another good means of communicating with you.

Agenda Setting

You and your client will go over the ten-question self-assessment that he completed from the preview section of his manual. You will also ask him what he would like to share from the writing in his Therapy Journal. (For more information on examining the self-assessment and the Therapy Journal, review "Agenda Setting" in session 3.)

In developing the agenda for this session, ask your client about those significant life problems that cause him to feel anxiety. If he has difficulty identifying such topics, explore with him any issues where he finds himself procrastinating or avoiding. At the same time, make note for yourself of those life issues that your client has effectively dealt with. In looking at his problem-solving abilities he is likely to underestimate those skills he already possesses. After all, anxiety tends to downplay our sense of our own resources and to emphasize the intensity of the threat. You can use these instances of your client's constructive problem solving to help illustrate those principles you will discuss in this session and to encourage him if he feels like giving up.

Specific goals for this session include:

1. Reviewing homework from session 4

2. Educating the client about problem solving and guiding him through an in-session problem-solving exercise

3. Educating him about adding Adaptive Response to his weekly Thought Record

4. Exploring correlations between his personal relationships and his problem-solving skills

Review of Homework from Session 4

How did your client respond to daily risk assessments? Of the therapy skills covered in treating GAD, this one takes less time and seems to be less threatening; there seem to be fewer internal reasons that block this homework. Did your client learn new aspects of threat that he did not recognize at first? This is a common experience for clients who undertake risk assessment. As the anxious person begins to look at his life in detail he often finds unexpected areas of perceived danger. These are likely to be subtle, so your careful questioning can help bring these qualities to light.

Your client may conclude that his areas of risk are somehow silly or trivial. For example, "It's stupid for me to worry about being criticized at work because my performance is always excellent." Obviously, excellent performance does not overrule the worry of being criticized. As a matter of fact, an underlying fear of criticism may be what drives the individual to excellence in the first place. Be prepared to stand up for the legitimacy of a perceived risk that your client is ready to dismiss as silly or stupid. Anxiety is full of risks that may appear superficially illogical or irrational, but that makes them no less real. If this attitude is significantly entrenched for your client, his tendency to discount risks that seem trivial to him will take time to soften and change. Through your reclaiming those disowned risks, you can gradually help him see them as an indisputable part of himself as well as a valuable source of insight into his anxiety. Once they are recognized as legitimate, he can then begin the real therapeutic work of laying these particular risks to rest—as will be detailed in later sessions (especially session 6).

How did your client do with the PMR-8 practice? Did he notice a difference from the full PMR? If so, specific methods from the full PMR could be introduced to the shorter version. Most clients like the convenience of the PMR-8. Does this feature make it more likely that your client will use relaxation after the immediate homework is complete?

Concepts and Skills

Psychoeducation

Problem Solving

Your client is likely to believe that his own capacity for problem solving is defective, whether that is actually true or not. An anxious person typically feels that he is not able to solve problems well. This may align with other perceived deficits on his part so that he carries a core belief in his own lack of competence.

For there to be real gains in overcoming anxiety, your client needs to feel a greater sense of confidence in his ability to solve the life problems that come his way. This comes in part by learning and practicing one simple method of dealing with problems that will be outlined here. There will be plenty of opportunity to put this to use during the session and in the days that follow. But every bit as important is for the client to walk away with a greater understanding and respect for his problem solving that he has been using all along. The extent to which an anxious client will degrade in his mind what he is capable of doing is tragic. People with anxiety naturally overlook their considerable resourcefulness and how they have dealt successfully with very difficult circumstances. You have an opportunity to bring these abilities to light and give them the recognition they deserve. Over time your client can learn to revise his view of his history as well as to give himself credit for the resources he brings to bear in his present life.

Hopefully, in the sessions leading up to this one you have been listening for the client to tell you about his attempts at problem solving. Learn what methods he favors. Not only will this better help you explain problem solving in a way that will make sense to him, but you can better reinforce the problem solving he has been doing all along. You'll probably notice that once he had undertaken risk assessment he was spontaneously heading toward problem solving. An indication of whether risk is viewed in its accurate form is the individual's resulting tendency to take action that reduces the level of the risk. Valid perception naturally leads to necessary response.

Skill Building

Guiding Your Client through In-Session Problem Solving

In this session you will be guiding your client in learning a particular approach to solving problems as developed by D'Zurilla and Goldfried (1971). Their method is both simple and easy to remember. Essentially, there are five steps (though for the purposes of this session three more are included below—steps 1, 2, and 8), easily remembered with the acronym SOLVE:

State your problem
Outline your goals
List your alternatives
View the consequences
Evaluate your results

1. **Pick a Situation That Causes Moderate Anxiety**

   Ask your client to pick a situation that causes moderate anxiety, defined as 40 or 50 on a scale of 100—certainly not more than 60. You want him to practice problem solving in a situation that has a good chance of success. There shouldn't be too much anxiety because it is difficult to learn something new when he feels a lot of worry. If he is in doubt, tell him to start with a less anxious situation.

2. **Think about the Worst Possible Outcome**

   Ask him to use his risk assessment to consider what the worst possible outcome would look like. He should make it personal to him, not just a general statement of what would be awful for most people. He should provide as much emotional detail as possible. This is what really brings it to life.

3. **State the Problem**

   The problem is what blocks him from getting what he wants or what would be good for him. "I'm terribly self-conscious around members of the opposite sex." It may be the kind of interference that causes pain for him or for his loved ones. "I live in a bad neighborhood where I worry about my family all the time." The problem usually carries with it strong emotion as a signal that things are not okay. When he feels anxious, angry, confused, or depressed, these may be the messages that there exists a blockage from getting what would be good for him.

4. **Outline the Goals**

   What are his goals for change? These are the aspects of himself or his immediate experience that he wants to be different. These might include a change in his feelings, in his thoughts or attitudes, or in his actions. Tell him to think of the goal as being the positive growth to get beyond his particular situation.

5. **List the Alternatives**

   Now is the time for him to come up with as many possible solutions as he can think of. He shouldn't worry about whether or not they would actually work. That question comes later. Tell him to be as open and bold as he can because new approaches are necessary for him to break free of his old ways of thinking about the problem. The more alternatives, the better.

6. **View the Consequences**

   This is where he selects his most promising alternatives and views the consequences of putting them into action. He should start by choosing the single goal from step 4 that is most attractive to him. Ask him to cross out those possible alternatives that are obviously wrong for the situation. Whenever possible he should combine several approaches into one strategy, which will be his plan of action. Under each strategy he will list possible positive and negative consequences for himself and the other people involved. What are the short-range and long-range implications?

7. **Evaluate the Results**

   As this session comes to a close, it is time to help your client plan for problem-solving in his day-to-day life (he will practice steps 1 through 8 at home). You want to encourage him to take what has been learned from this session and apply it in his real experience. Ask him to try to maintain a balance of hoping for positive outcomes while not being too disappointed if things don't turn out perfectly. In undertaking something new he has an ideal opportunity to learn about himself and his situation. Most often his attempt at a solution will fix some of the problems while bringing other issues to his attention. Tell him to give himself credit for what he has accomplished so far.

8. **Rerate the Anxiety**

   After your client has completed step 7 during his at-home practice, he will have, hopefully, realized some reduction in his anxiety. If not, there may be remaining issues that have not been resolved. Before the close of this session, let him know that this is a possibility and tell him that if this is the case he should try a risk assessment to see what may seem threatening. Sometimes more serious problems remain hidden until the smaller ones are out of the way. He may discover newfound anxiety about himself as a problem solver. Does he fail to live up to his own expectations? Is he running the risk of going beyond what he expected of himself in solving problems? These will be important issues to explore with him.

Adaptive Response

What your client has learned in this session about problem solving will become an important part of how he continues to make gains on his anxiety. By the conclusion of his treatment the hope would be that when he encounters a disturbing situation, distressing feelings, or troubling thoughts, he would attempt some type of reaction intended to change those negative conditions. CBT calls this process the adaptive response. The essence of therapy is assisting our clients to feel capable of making adaptive responses to the wide variety of challenges they face in their lives. When a client who has been struggling with GAD can consistently make adaptive responses to the sources of his anxiety, his GAD will be essentially resolved.

"Adaptive Response" will be the final feature you will add to your client's weekly Thought Record. It takes its logical place following the client's own view of his "Worst Outcome." Sometimes the client's adaptive response will be problem solving, and that's why adaptive response is described in this chapter. Depending upon the specifics of the triggering situation, a client may draw upon other therapy skills learned so far, including relaxation or risk assessment. The remaining therapy skills to be learned over the course of treatment will also be types of adaptive response.

Obviously, when writing this portion of his Thought Record the client will describe in personal terms how he applied the adaptive response. For example, "used relaxation for five minutes, then made my risk assessment when I was no longer freaked out." Adaptive response combines the various methods discussed over the course of treatment with all the other skills the client has learned in his life. Adaptive response is a very broad category, the essence of which is that we can actively move forward in dealing with the issues that trouble ourselves and our loved ones.

Following is an example of the form, now including "Adaptive Response," that your client will fill out this week and in all successive sessions.

Thought Record

Triggering Situation	Anxiety and Other Feelings	Automatic Thoughts	Worst Outcome	Adaptive Response	Rerate Feelings and Thoughts

Daily Worry Record: Week Four

Date	Average Level of Anxiety	Peak Level of Anxiety
_____	_____	_____
_____	_____	_____
_____	_____	_____
_____	_____	_____
_____	_____	_____
_____	_____	_____
_____	_____	_____
_____	_____	_____
_____	_____	_____
_____	_____	_____
_____	_____	_____
_____	_____	_____
_____	_____	_____
_____	_____	_____
_____	_____	_____
_____	_____	_____
_____	_____	_____
_____	_____	_____
_____	_____	_____
_____	_____	_____

Personal Relationships and Problem Solving

With whom does the client feel competent? Where can he recognize that his problem-solving ability is supported and appreciated? These are likely to be among his healthier relationships and provide a sense of the direction in which he wants to grow. He may also need to confront the fact that certain people likely undercut his sense of being able to solve problems. They may obscure his view of the initial problem so he's not clear what he's dealing with. Or they may seek to block his goals, giving the impression that what he wants would not be feasible or desirable. We've all heard, at one time or another, "That would certainly be selfish to want such and such for yourself." Others can also interfere in the processes of viewing valid options, undertaking some kind of action, or taking stock of the results. As the client gains more practice in problem solving, he can begin to notice who in his life supports these developments and who seems to block them. This can bring to light what may be current relationship problems as well as provide clues to where in his past the undercutting had its origins. Steps can then be taken in therapy to reduce the negative impact of these problems and their origins.

Session Summary

Briefly summarize the material covered in the session. Try to reflect those learning points personally notable to your client. If your client disagrees with or seems to not understand your summary, you should ask him questions to find out why.

Feedback from Client

At the conclusion of each session, ask your client for feedback about the usefulness of the material and any questions that may remain. Encourage him to give feedback so that you can address any concerns that may have arisen.

Homework for This Session

1. Ask your client to practice problem solving on a daily basis. This makes sense to most clients. Remind him to be aware of his internal process as he is going through the process. Is he discovering negative beliefs about his ability to deal with the situation? Does he have strong doubts his process will have a favorable outcome? Is he discouraged by having too few alternatives, or does he feel overwhelmed by having too many? This is all essential material for the client to be recording on a day-by-day basis in his Therapy Journal. Only a portion of a homework experience is intended to teach the client a new skill. Every bit as important is the fresh internal awareness that occurs in the early stages of doing something out of the ordinary.

2. Your client is now in his third week of relaxation techniques. This time, he will guide himself through shorthand muscle relaxation (his instructions are in his manual). Remind him that as he gains skills in relaxation techniques he will be able to graduate to methods that more quickly move him to a relaxed state.

3. Ask your client to take the STAI between now and the next session. This is to assess where his anxiety stands at approximately the midpoint of therapy. As much as possible he should respond to his most current feelings and experiences and not think how he filled out the test the first time. Once it is completed he can compare his present scores with how he felt at the beginning of therapy. Hopefully there are some areas of improvement, but certain issues of concern may remain. You and your client can discuss these matters in detail and determine how to use the time left in therapy to make sure headway is gained.

4. Remind him to complete his Daily Worry Record as well as his Thought Record, which now describes in personal terms how he applied the adaptive response. He should bring his records with him to the next session.

5. Remind him to read the "Preview to Session 6" that appears in his manual. As discussed in session 2, he will need to complete the ten-question self-assessment that appears in that section of his manual and bring it with him to the next session with you.

Session 6

Worry Exposure

Monitoring of Current Status

Again, begin by asking the client whether any significant concerns—related to therapy or otherwise—have arisen since the previous session. Remember to try to keep this early discussion under ten minutes. (You may want to review "Monitoring of Current Status" in session 2.)

You and your client will discuss the Worry Record that she kept over the course of the last week so that you can get a sense of her current level of anxiety. (For more details on examining this record, review "Monitoring of Current Status" in session 3.)

In your client's second week of completing a Thought Record along with her Worry Record, is she beginning to see how the two records coordinate? The situation involving "Peak Level of Anxiety" on the Worry Record is usually a good opportunity for a Thought Record. Is your client noticing any changes in her level of anxiety before and after completing a Thought Record? Over time the majority of people experience some relief in their anxiety by going through this process. If this is not the case yet for your client, you can troubleshoot to see if there are any obvious problems that can explain why she is not getting some relief. You can also reassure her that even if she doesn't feel better at the present, there is much to be learned from completing Thought Records and the feeling of relief will come in the not-too-distant future.

This is the first time that your client has made a deliberate adaptive response to deal with her anxiety. What kinds of early experience did she have? If the results are favorable you can share your positive regard and congratulations in a quiet way. No need to go overboard. If the results are negative, you and your client will analyze what happened and see what can be learned. Is she discouraged or demoralized? You might reinforce for her that the therapeutic emphasis is really on the effort rather than the results. Through this effort a person feels less passive in the face of her anxiety. She is learning and growing based upon these new experiences. With this outlook, positive results will eventually come.

Agenda Setting

You and your client will go over the ten-question self-assessment that she completed from the preview section of her manual. You will also ask her what she would like to share from the writing in her Therapy Journal. (For more information on examining the self-assessment and the Therapy Journal, review "Agenda Setting" in session 3.)

At this point in the therapy you should have a good sense of the main worry topics in your client's life, and you will also likely have enough experience working with her to know the topics she tends to underestimate or avoid. After she has spontaneously generated her worry items, see if there are any remaining from your own list. This doesn't happen often, but when it does it can lead to your client feeling embarrassment. You can help ease this negative reaction by reminding the client that anxiety tends to block our clear view of things—particularly those things that make us anxious.

Specific goals for this session include:

1. Reviewing homework from session 5

2. Educating the client about worry and guiding her through an in-session worry-exposure exercise

3. Exploring correlations between her personal relationships and her tendency to worry

Review of Homework from Session 5

How did your client do with problem solving? In following the steps of this simple method did she arrive at solutions she had felt herself incapable of? Could she accept these as legitimate or did she somehow discount them? For example, "I was able to solve easy problems for homework, but real issues from my actual life still overwhelm me." See if you can demonstrate to the client how these underlying beliefs undercut what she has accomplished. Does this occur in other areas of her life? How does this affect her feelings about herself as well as her readiness to take on problems?

In practicing problem solving, the client often recognizes other ways that she solves problems in day-to-day life but had not acknowledged. An anxious person may have a belief about herself that she is ineffectual and that she cannot deal with her problems. While it may be helpful to teach the client new skills, more important is to help her really grasp the range of problems she already deals with. Can she experiment with feeling slightly less anxious while generating a greater sense of confidence that she can handle more and more of what comes her way?

What kind of results did your client get from shorthand muscle relaxation? She should be gaining more confidence that she can consistently bring herself to a more relaxed state. Is she finding this practice pleasurable? If there are problems, can you identify the types of anxious thoughts and feelings that get in her way?

You'll be interpreting your client's midtherapy STAI results in this session. Pay attention not only to the objective changes compared to the initial measure, but also gauge how she is responding during session to what it shows about her level current of anxiety. Is she encouraged, disappointed, proud of herself, or frustrated? Suggest that she share her reactions with you. This becomes a good opportunity to discuss with each other what has worked and not worked in the therapy to date, with an eye toward making necessary adjustments. It also sets the stage for you and the client to further focus on what remaining anxiety issues will be most important to work on between now and the end of therapy.

Concepts and Skills

Psychoeducation

Worry Revisited

With anxiety there is a natural tendency to avoid what seems to be the origins of the threats. This accounts for the strong link between anxiety and avoidance. Unless your client can interrupt this cycle she will not make much headway with her GAD.

Worry exposure is the most effective means of reducing her tendency to avoid. With your help and support, she will be encouraged to confront rather than avoid the sources of her threats. Over time this not only extinguishes the avoidance response, but also helps habituate her to her anxiety. Hopefully, she'll see a decrease in the negative impact that her anxious response—that once seemed so overwhelming—has on her, if it's simply endured. Anxiety then loses enough of its sting to become just another regular life circumstance to be taken care of like anything else.

In this session your client will learn to use her imagination for generating the sources of her threat. This provides her with more control over how she wants to set up and manage the exposure, compared to the less predictable nature of real-life events. With proper guidance from you, the resulting experience can be every bit as vivid for her as actual events.

On par with relaxation, worry exposure is one of the most important therapy skills for overcoming GAD that she will learn. There is nothing more effective in rooting out the anxious tendency to avoid the source of threat. Because of the benefits derived from this particular skill, she will practice worry exposure for two to four weeks. If there is not enough progress after one session, you and she might decide to add an additional session to her therapy plan to make sure worry exposure is covered sufficiently.

Can you get a sense of your client's capacity for imagination? You might consider how she has done with relaxation (session 2), worst outcome (session 3), and generating alternatives (session 4) to gauge to what extent she can internally generate and hold an image. If she seems to have an aptitude in this area, you can encourage her based upon her earlier accomplishments and she is likely to do well. If imagination seems not to be a comfortable arena for her, you may consider why. Does she think it necessary to be always factual and concrete? Does she get nervous if she strays beyond the literal? Drawing upon your therapeutic skill you may seek to reassure her that you and she can start with the real while also developing toward the imaginary. She may then be able to better see the value in this experience by your integrating it with creativity and opportunity. To the extent that you are successful, she may be able to set aside her anxious attachment to the factual world and begin to experience some of the value of her internal life.

Skill Building

Guiding Your Client through Worry Exposure

1. **List the Worries**

   Ask your client to think about all the situations that make her feel anxious. She should write a list that includes the events from her past that continue to cause her anxiety as well as possible circumstances in her future that she worries about. She may include concerns about personal rejection, making mistakes, disappointing someone else, physical illness, harm to herself or someone she cares about, and so on. Suggest that she go back through the "Assessing Yourself" questionnaires from her previews to see if additional worries come to mind.

2. **Rank the Worries**

   Next, your client will pick the item that causes her the least anxiety and place it at the top of a new list. She'll select the next least distressing worry and place it in the second position, and will proceed until her new list ranks all her worries from the least anxiety-provoking to the most anxiety-provoking. If she can't decide between two items that seem to cause her equal worry, tell her to go with her first impression. She can always revise the order later.

3. **Relax**

   Now she should prepare to work with the first item on her worry list by getting into a comfortable position, breathing deeply, and beginning her cue-controlled relaxation. Tell her to let stress and tension flow out of her body. While it's best for her to keep her eyes closed, if this is really uncomfortable she may try it for short periods at first and develop familiarity over time.

4. **Imagine a Worry and Begin Exposure**

   The client should bring to mind her first worry, using all her senses to make the image sharp and clear. She wants to be able to see the details as they unfold, from beginning, to middle, to end. She should try to hear those associated sounds that would automatically bring a shock or a chill to her body. Tell her to play the scene like a movie that runs over and over again to the worst possible outcome. See if she can view the movie in slow motion so that her mental time is delayed. The experience needs to be as vivid as possible.

   It will be especially important for her to imagine the physical sensations of her worry. Ask her, "In your mind can you recreate the churning of your stomach? The painful tightness in your shoulders? The damp skin of your arm pits? Your cold hands that can never seem to warm up?"

   She should try to stay focused on the worry image for twenty-five minutes. If she finds distracting thoughts coming in, help her gently bring herself back to the worry image. There is a natural tendency to avoid the sources of anxiety and it may take some practice for her to develop the skills to remain focused.

5. **Rate the Peak Anxiety**

   In the midst of her imagining, ask her to rate her highest anxiety, using a rating scale from 0 for no anxiety to 100 for the worst she's experienced.

6. **Imagine Alternative Outcomes**

   After she's finished the full twenty-five-minute worry exposure, tell her to imagine *different* outcomes that carry less stress. This step shouldn't be started too early, or she will lose the benefit from the worry exposure. As before, she should use a range of physical senses when she imagines scenes of resolution, satisfaction, comfort, or protection. She may find it interesting to introduce a playful or magical quality to some of the alternatives. This wrap-up should last at least five minutes, but can run longer if your client wishes.

7. **Rerate the Anxiety**

After five minutes of the alternative outcomes, ask her to rerate her anxiety. It will probably be lower than the previous rating.

Personal Relationships and Worry Exposure

This new skill, one of the most important of the entire therapy, opens doors that were once shut. The client has likely been avoiding all kinds of things, while still feeling more and more anxious. With worry exposure the client is beginning to face and explore what once seemed too frightening. Where does this lead in terms of the client's personal relationships? What may have been avoided there? Perhaps it was instances of interpersonal conflict that felt too dangerous to the client, as though someone might be annihilated in the process. Maybe it was circumstances of intimacy that caused the client to feel too vulnerable in the attraction to or rejection of a loved one. Perhaps she felt wariness of true cooperation with another person, somehow fearing it would involve an obligation that she would inevitably fail to perform properly. Whatever the case, worry exposure carries many implications for the personal relationships of the client.

Session Summary

Briefly summarize the material covered in the session. Try to reflect those learning points personally notable to your client. If your client disagrees with or seems to not understand your summary, you should ask her questions to find out why.

Feedback from Client

At the conclusion of each session, ask your client for feedback about the usefulness of the material and any questions that may remain. Encourage her to give feedback so that you can address any concerns that may have arisen.

Homework for This Session

1. Ask the client to practice worry exposure every day for the next two to four weeks. This should give her sufficient time to work through each step of the hierarchy she has constructed. She should write her hierarchy in detail in her Therapy Journal and take daily notes about her exposure process. Help your client see the value of spending adequate time going through this process rather than trying to take a shortcut. There cannot be long-term relief from the worry stimuli unless there is sufficient time spent in exposure to them. Remind your

client that, in addition to relaxation, this is the most important therapy skill she will be learning.

2. Your client is now in her final phase of self-guided relaxation. This week, she will practice the cue-controlled relaxation described in her manual.

3. Remind her to complete her Daily Worry Record and Thought Record and bring the records with her to the next session.

4. Remind her to read the "Preview to Session 7" that appears in her manual. As discussed in session 2, she will need to complete the ten-question self-assessment that appears in that section of the manual and bring it with her to the next session with you.

Session 7

Reducing Safety Behaviors

Monitoring of Current Status

Again, begin by asking the client whether any significant concerns—related to therapy or otherwise—have arisen since the previous session. Remember to try to keep this early discussion under ten minutes. (You may want to review "Monitoring of Current Status" in session 2.)

You and your client will discuss the Worry Record and Thought Record that he kept over the course of the last week so that you can get a sense of his current level of anxiety. (For more details on examining these two documents, review "Monitoring of Current Status" in sessions 3, 5, and 6.)

Is the client feeling comfortable coordinating the Worry Records and Thought Records? Since treatment is approximately two thirds complete at this point you should be noticing a reduction of anxiety on the Worry Record from week to week. The Thought Records ought to be reflecting a decrease in anxiety before and after the record was done. Does your client seem more confident in generating adaptive responses in the face of anxiety? Are there blind spots or remaining problems that should be brought into the agenda?

Agenda Setting

You and your client will go over the ten-question self-assessment that he completed from the preview section of his manual. You will also ask him what he would like to share from the writing in his Therapy Journal. (For more information on examining the self-assessment and the Therapy Journal, review "Agenda Setting" in session 3.)

As you and your client develop agenda for this session, discuss the things he does to try to ease his anxiety. What does he see to be the pros and the cons of each approach? Does he remember when he first started these behaviors? Have him imagine what it would be like for him not to be driven by these behaviors. Can you help him develop what this personal future would look like? The main goal in this session is to strip away the automatic nature of these behaviors and have the client really think about which are worth keeping versus which he should get rid of.

Specific goals for this session include:

1. Reviewing homework from session 6

2. Educating the client about safety behaviors and guiding him through an in-session practice

3. Exploring correlations between his personal relationships and his safety behaviors

Review of Homework from Session 6

Follow up on your client's worry exposure and see how he is doing with his list of items. It would not be surprising if new items come forward for his list, either from his personal life or in session with you.

Worry exposure is at the heart of overcoming GAD. What kinds of experiences is your client having? If he feels some relief after having gone through a full worry exposure, he can actually see the benefit of this method. Perhaps he has noticed that confronting and sticking with the anxious image makes it gradually loses its power. Clients often experience a quality of excitement and describe feeling a newfound sense of freedom. These early successes usually reinforce an individual's desire to keep moving down his list toward the most anxiety-provoking item.

If your client has not had early success, you and he want to figure out why. Perhaps the items he attempted were too tame or too dangerous. Or perhaps he has not developed full skills in generating images of anxious material. Or it might be that he grew frightened of this extended exposure to a threatening image and bailed out before he could expect to feel real relief (requiring approximately twenty to twenty-five minutes). If any of these explanations apply, you can best help your client by starting over with the process and reconstructing it step by step. Try very hard to prevent him from quitting worry exposure. Running away from failed worry exposures leaves a sense of defeat and futility.

Did your client have success in using cue-controlled relaxation in the face of real anxiety? Were there occasions when he thought about using it, but decided not to? If so, why didn't he? Whereas all the relaxation exercises up to this point are generally helpful with anxiety, cue-controlled relaxation is the strongest in helping with the raw and immediate reaction to an anxiety situation. Remind him that the method is sufficiently private that he can use it during an anxiety trigger and not feel self-conscious.

Concepts and Skills

Psychoeducation

Safety Behaviors

Safety behaviors are maintained by the same psychology that reinforces superstitious behavior. When we come to believe that a certain behavior makes a bad situation better, we can be powerfully persuaded to do it again—and again, and again. And if every time we do it we also tell ourselves that it has improved the situation, our chain of behavior becomes even more ingrained. Underlying most anxiety there is a whole trail of safety behaviors in which we are convinced that our actions save us from a worse outcome. This assumption is typically unexamined and untested.

With the skill referred to as "reducing safety behaviors," we want to simply see where the truth stands. Let actual experience tell your client what really makes him safer and when there exists only an illusion of safety. To do this he needs to begin to set aside some of his safety behaviors, starting with the ones that feel least essential to his status quo. Perhaps you'll choose to work on your patterns of checking the lock four times before he leaves the house, or calling his wife throughout the day to make sure she is okay, or arriving at work a half hour early to be certain he is not behind when he starts. By slowly dispensing with his safety behaviors he can test where there remains a real need for concern and where he can afford to relax. This will likely be a challenge for him. Should he find himself falling back into old safety-behavior habits, suggest that he look at it as a source of amusement as well as a reminder of how ingrained the behaviors are. Then urge him to begin again, immediately, to reduce the safety behavior he has targeted.

Hopefully, during your previous work with your client you've been aware of where and when he used safety behaviors in hopes of reducing his anxiety. Ideally, you've been quietly collecting evidence of situations where they seemed to work effectively for him as well as when there appeared to be no benefit. As you and the client begin to explore these consequences during the session this week, he may feel embarrassed or ashamed of these "silly" things he does. Don't overlook this. Addressing his negative reaction is important as it likely reflects a pattern of similar feelings toward his more vulnerable areas. As this discussion unfolds you might also explore whether he can get in touch with a sense of compassion for his actions. Depending on how the therapeutic relationship has developed you may choose to share your personal reaction to his (and your own) tendencies in this area. It might help to remind him that whatever exists today as safety behaviors originated as adaptive response in the face of what felt like overwhelming circumstances. These reactions were his best attempt to deal with an earlier situation that was beyond his control. While he likely feels just as insecure now, in fact he is probably much more capable than when the pattern began. Finally getting the safety behaviors out of the way then becomes a relief, allowing additional progress to be made.

Skill Building

Working on Safety Behaviors during the Session

1. **List the Safety Behaviors**

   You and your client are going to compose a list during this session. First, ask him to think about all the things he does in hopes of reducing the chronic worry in his life. These habits have developed to keep bad things from happening. It might be triple-checking all of his work, or washing his hands each time he touches someone, or phoning to check on his family numerous times a day. Many times these habits become so familiar he doesn't even notice anymore the many ways he tries to cover his anxiety. Help him write a list of all such behaviors.

2. **Identify the Easiest Behavior to Stop, and Predict the Consequences of Doing So**
   What behavior could he reduce with the least amount of harm to himself and people around him? Ask him to make a prediction based upon his realistic view of the evidence. What are the possible consequences? What are the likely consequences?

3. **Imagine Stopping the Easiest Behavior**
   This is where he begins to test the prediction during session. Ask him to imagine the situation in detail and exactly how his safety behavior would fit in. Can he really get a feeling for what that would feel like? Now he should imagine stopping the behavior and seeing what happens. Did his anxiety lead him to be too pessimistic? Did his hope for relief make him too optimistic?

4. **Check the Anxiety Before and After**
   His anxiety will likely rise at first when he imagines resisting a safety behavior, even when it is one of the easier on his list. This can remind him of the power behind the safety behaviors and why they are so ingrained. If he can resist long enough to see that the worst outcome doesn't automatically happen, he can begin to reduce his anxiety. It becomes possible to think about living free of the obligations and restrictions imposed by your anxiety.

5. **Repeat the Steps for the Next Hardest Behavior**
   The real gains in dealing with GAD come from building upon initial successes. Based upon his progress handling the easiest safety behavior, he may want to move forward to the next hardest.

Working on Safety Behaviors out of Session

Your client will take the same process he practiced in his imagination during session and apply it to his day-to-day life. He will follow each of the previous steps, but will resist doing the actual behavior, rather than just imagining it. The hardest part of the technique will likely be letting the situation unfold without jumping in with his customary safety behaviors. It will probably help him to substitute a new (and less anxiety-driven) behavior. This way he can aim for a better response to the situation at hand as well as steer clear of the anguish of doing absolutely nothing in the face of something he worries about.

Remind your client that safety behaviors have a long half-life and do not go away easily. Tell him not to be surprised if he notices a tendency for his old safety behaviors to drift back into place. The people who originally benefited from his safety behaviors may try new ways to get him to take over worrying on their behalf. Or he might notice that he starts accumulating alternate safety behaviors to fill the empty place left by the old ones.

In any case, the methods he used to make headway with the original safety behavior will work again. Remind him of the good feeling he had when he made progress in setting aside some safety behaviors.

Personal Relationships and Reducing Safety Behaviors

The safety behaviors of your client are likely to be closely linked with the people in his life. At times it may be because of his concern for them that he engages in safety behaviors—the behaviors are actually on behalf of those people. Or perhaps it may be due to their worry about him that *they* are the ones who undertake their own safety behaviors. These connections can be entangled and enmeshed. Boundaries between one person and the next get a bit murky. As your client in therapy begins to hold back from his safety behaviors to see what really happens as a result, he can also start to explore where these entanglements exist between him and other people. Who is really worried about whom? For whose benefit is the safety behavior? Much is likely to come to light from this line of thought.

Do you recognize whether there have been safety behaviors enacted between you and your client in the therapeutic relationship? It is not uncommon that one or the other or both of you engage in certain activities hoping to make the union feel safer. Keep your eyes open as to what you notice. Raise the question with your client and see if he is aware of anything you haven't identified yet.

Session Summary

Briefly summarize the material covered in the session. Try to reflect those learning points personally notable to your client. If your client disagrees with or seems to not understand your summary, you should ask him questions to find out why.

Feedback from Client

At the conclusion of each session, ask your client for feedback about the usefulness of the material and any questions that may remain. Encourage him to give feedback so that you can address any concerns that may have arisen.

Homework for This Session

1. Ask your client to practice reducing his safety behaviors daily. It usually doesn't require much more than a week to see progress. He should keep good notes in his Therapy Journal, with particular attention to the early impact of this new skill on his personal relationships. The client may notice some individuals in his life who start to become really uncomfortable when he reduces his safety behaviors. These people have likely grown to depend on the client as a person who provides safety or responsibility. What happens when those duties are not automatically performed? Is it time to renegotiate what some of the expectations have been? Does the relationship feel any better when some of the safety behaviors are set aside?

2. This will be your client's second week of practice with worry exposure. This week, he'll be proceeding to the next step: now that he has made gains in worry exposure via his imagination he can begin the same process in vivo (in real life). Again guided by his list, he can begin to select low-stress circumstances in which to place himself. He wants to expose himself to his worry in the real world so that he gains greater confidence in his ability to tolerate the resulting feelings. Remind him not to try to solve the problem he is confronting. That may sound odd to him, but while it is a useful approach in other areas, here we want the triggering situation to go on long enough so that he has the experience of habituating to the anxiety. That would likely not happen if he stepped in and solved it right away. With repeated exposures he will probably be feeling less anxious, and at that later time there would be no reason why he should not solve the problem straight away. Ask him to write about this process in detail in his Therapy Journal.

3. Remind him to complete his Daily Worry Record and Thought Record and bring the records with him to the next session.

4. Remind him to read the "Preview To Session 8" that appears in his manual. As discussed in session 2, he will need to complete the ten-question self-assessment that appears in that section of the manual and bring it with him to the next session with you.

Thought-Stopping

Monitoring of Current Status

Again, begin by asking the client whether any significant concerns—related to therapy or otherwise—have arisen since the previous session. Remember to try to keep this early discussion under ten minutes. (You may want to review "Monitoring of Current Status" in session 2.)

You and your client will discuss the Worry Record and Thought Record that she kept over the course of the last week so that you can get a sense of her current level of anxiety. (For more details on examining these two documents, review "Monitoring of Current Status" in sessions 3, 5, and 6.)

Agenda Setting

You and your client will go over the ten-question self-assessment that she completed from the preview section of her manual. You will also ask her what she would like to share from the writing in her Therapy Journal. (For more information on examining the self-assessment and the Therapy Journal, review "Agenda Setting" in session 3.)

You and your client will collect those repetitive automatic thoughts that have been surfacing over and over in session and in her Thought Records. By now these should be quite familiar to you both. In setting the agenda for this session, pay particular attention to the automatic thoughts that, though your client has done good therapy work in challenging the ideas, seem to keep coming back anyway. Do you see situations during your client's most recent week when such thoughts surfaced? Better yet, see if you can identify them when they occur during the session itself.

Specific goals for this session include:

1. Reviewing homework from session 7

2. Educating the client about thought-stopping and guiding her through an in-session practice

3. Exploring correlations between her personal relationships and thought-stopping

Review of Homework from Session 7

Because only a week is usually required to see progress on reducing safety behaviors, your client should have made significant gains by now. Having experimented with reducing safety behaviors, has the client determined what she would like to do in the long term? She may think it would require too much effort to contain these behaviors on an ongoing basis. If so, you can share your clinical experience to the effect that over time it becomes easier to leave the old behaviors behind. Remind her that if she wants to make such changes, for best effect she should plan in advance how to keep practicing.

Did your client practice in-vivo worry exposure? How did it go for her in making the transition from worry images to worry in real life? If problems arose, you should troubleshoot with her: perhaps she took on too much exposure too soon, or perhaps she needs some more work with worry images before progressing to real life. If your client is really demoralized, have her move back down her list to worry images that she already succeeded with that gave her confidence. This allows her to rebuild a sense of mastery that she can carry forward to the more challenging worry exposures.

Concepts and Skills

Psychoeducation

Thought-Stopping

By this point in therapy your client will have already analyzed, explored, and challenged all kinds of anxious thoughts and is probably seeing substantial progress. But still, occasionally, she'll find that the unwanted thoughts do not go away altogether. That's when the simple method of thought-stopping can allow your client to quickly shift to a more pleasant state of mind.

Thought-stopping was developed for treatment of obsessions and has proven helpful for obsessive individuals who can have lots and lots of unwanted thoughts. Thought-stopping is different from what would be an attempt to control thoughts. This process recognizes that for a variety of reasons, certain thoughts are going to appear. It is really not possible to alter that fact. But we still can have significant influence on our overall mental state based upon how we respond to our thoughts. We may choose to listen to them, challenge them, or stop them. Each choice affects the trail of thoughts that come behind it. Ask your client to think of it as "thought influencing" rather than "thought control."

Collect a sample of unwanted thoughts from sessions, the Therapy Journal, and Thought Records. Most people have a specific few that keep coming up over and over. Starting with these you and your client can build a list of unwanted thoughts to work with in session.

Part of the process involves the client yelling "Stop!" during the session as she is learning the technique. Sometimes people feel self-conscious raising their voices. If this is the case for your client, perhaps you can help her feel less inhibited by your modeling the method yourself. Make sure that you really belt it out. Do it several times. There'll probably be some nervous laughter between you and your client, and then she will likely feel less inhibited to do it on her own. If she still has a hard time with this, you can suggest that she use her regular volume in session and full voice at home. The point is to help the client get started in whatever way she feels comfortable, and then she can find what works best for her from there.

Skill Building

Guiding Your Client through In-Session Thought-Stopping

1. **List the Unwanted Thoughts**

   At this point in her therapy your client is probably quite familiar with her unwanted thoughts—they have appeared over and over in her Thought Records. Ask her to write down three or four using the exact language in which they appear in her mind. Then ask her to imagine a scene that would be likely to trigger that thought for her.

2. **List the Pleasant Thoughts**

   Ask her to list three thoughts that are distinctly pleasurable for her. Rather than making something up, she should try to identify actual thoughts that she really enjoys in her day-to-day life. They may be special memories about family outings, sporting events she's attended, favorite musical performances, or recognition she has earned. Or they may be repeated fantasies about a dream vacation, a hobby she'd like to learn, or a new sexual experience.

   Tell her it is best to generate new thoughts that have nothing to do with those that are unwanted. The point is not to challenge the thoughts that cause her pain or to replace them with something more realistic. For thought-stopping she simply wants to form pleasant thoughts that will move her to a preferred psychological place compared to where her unwanted thoughts left her.

3. **Relax and Entertain the Unwanted Thoughts**

   Begin thought-stopping when she is relaxed and calm. It will take some practice before she can apply it to the hot thoughts in her day-to-day life. Once she's comfortable, ask her to pick from her list of unwanted thoughts the thought and scene that bothers her the least. Start with this easy combination to develop her skills and confidence; she'll progress to the more difficult thoughts later. Ask her to close her eyes and focus on the negative thought and the scene for a few minutes. She should bring it into full distressing detail, including how it looks and sounds as the bad news unfolds. Ask her to be aware of possible discomfort in her body associated with the thought.

4. **Interrupt the Unwanted Thoughts**

   When her negative stream of thoughts and images is in full flow, she should shout "Stop!" out loud. Encourage her to really make a big noise. To accentuate the "Stop!" she can also open her eyes wide, jump out of her chair, raise her arms, and clap her hands loudly. If she seems embarrassed, remind her that there needs to be a strong physical interruption to break the obsessive train of thought. You can help her overcome any initial inhibitions by reassuring her that this is one of the most effective therapy techniques for dealing with GAD.

5. Switch to Pleasant Thoughts

Now ask her to dump those unpleasant thoughts and images immediately and jump into the pleasant scene. Give her the opportunity to enjoy the good feelings and positive sensations for a full thirty seconds. She should make this every bit as vivid as the unpleasant material. If she finds the unwanted thoughts intruding before the thirty seconds are complete, she should shout "Stop!" again and make them go away.

Your Client's Home Practice

As part of her homework, your client will repeat this exercise during relaxation in a quiet place. Once she can consistently shut down her least distressing unpleasant thought, she should move to the next most difficult one. She may find that pleasant thoughts and scenes fade over time or lose their positive power for her. At that time she should go to another from her list or develop fresh ones. She should continue with the loud shouts of "Stop!" until she can reliably halt the unwanted thoughts she generates during her quiet-time practice. She is then ready to progress to stating "Stop" in her normal voice while remaining seated in her chair. She will repeat the process until these statements consistently dispel the unwanted thoughts and allow her to switch to pleasant material. Next, she will practice "Stop" in a whisper.

When the whisper is enough, help her develop a subvocal method to "Stop." Tell her to imagine hearing herself shout "Stop!" accompanied by the sudden physical jolt created during her early practice. She should make the experience as real as possible by moving her vocal cords and tongue as if she were actually uttering the sound. As she develops confidence with this subvocal method, she can stop unwanted thoughts in public or when she is with other people. She need not make a sound nor draw attention to herself.

She is then ready to use thought stopping in her day-to-day life: when she becomes aware that she is obsessing, she will shout "Stop!" in her mind and switch to pleasant thoughts for a full thirty seconds. This may require that she takes a pause in her regular activities, but the time is well spent. It may call for a few additional attempts in the early stages to get the unwanted thought to stop completely, so remind her to try not to be impatient with herself.

She can also reinforce the "Stop" method by using physical interrupters. These are discreet methods to bring her body awareness into the process. She can wear a rubber band around her wrist and snap it to make an unwanted thought halt, or she can press her fingernail against her palm, or gently bite her tongue or cheek. Obviously she is not to cause herself pain, but simply issue a clear physical message to break through her chain of unwanted thoughts.

Remind her to try to catch an unwanted thought as soon as possible, because that is when it is most easily redirected and has caused her the least amount of aggravation. She should keep a ready supply of pleasant thoughts and images and move there quickly when the need arises.

Personal Relationships and Thought-Stopping

With this new skill the client is exploring what it means to put her foot down and say "No!" to her own unwanted thoughts. What are the implications of beginning to do the same in her personal relationships? More than likely she is a person who has been compliant with the expectations of other people. Such is the nature of anxiety. She has said "yes" to them for fear that something bad would happen if she objected. At this point in therapy it may be warranted for the client to reexamine her relationships and the various expectations, demands, and favors that she has felt obliged to meet. What happens if she decides that she no longer wants at least some of these expectations? Who can foresee the consequences when she begins to say "no"? Whose anxiety increases? Whose decreases? How can some of these expectations be renegotiated in ways that feel better to everyone?

Session Summary

Briefly summarize the material covered in the session. Try to reflect those learning points personally notable to your client. If your client disagrees with or seems to not understand your summary, you should ask her questions to find out why.

Feedback from Client

At the conclusion of each session, ask your client for feedback about the usefulness of the material and any questions that may remain. Encourage her to give feedback so that you can address any concerns that may have arisen.

Homework for This Session

1. You will ask your client to try thought-stopping at least once a day between now and the next session. Once the client gets the hang of it, thought-stopping can be fun. For a person who has been anxious for an extended period of time, it's nice for your client to be able to have some positive influence on what she thinks about on a moment-to-moment basis. Suggest she keep her Therapy Journal close at hand this week so she can document the small moments when she used thought-stopping and influenced her train of thought in a favorable way.

   Your client may wonder whether thought-stopping is just a glorified version of denial. You may assist her in reconsidering if these unwanted thoughts are really her avoidance of important material she needs to examine. In all likelihood, these thoughts have been examined up one side and down the other. What else is to be gained by thrashing them through every single time they appear?

2. Remind her to complete her Daily Worry Record and Thought Record and bring the records with her to the next session.

3. Remind her to read the "Preview to Session 9" that appears in her manual. As discussed in session 2, she will need to complete the ten-question self-assessment that appears in that section of the manual and bring it with her to the next session with you.

4. Ask your client to reread her Thought Records from the previous weeks in preparation for the next session. Have her pay attention to the main themes that emerge. Make sure that she brings her manual with her to session 9 as well as any additional Thought Records she has completed from photocopies.

5. Ask your client to complete the Program Satisfaction Questionnaire prior to next week's session. This will provide a written venue for you and your client to discuss the therapy you've done together. Remember, CBT is an information-rich therapeutic approach and this allows the sharing of feedback. It's a fine opportunity to learn more about yourself as a therapist through your client's experience of working with you.

Session 9

Revising Core Beliefs

Monitoring of Current Status

Again, begin by asking the client whether any significant concerns—related to therapy or otherwise—have arisen since the previous session. Remember to try to keep this early discussion under ten minutes. (You may want to review "Monitoring of Current Status" in session 2.)

You and your client will discuss the Worry Record and Thought Record that he kept over the course of the last week so that you can get a sense of his current level of anxiety. (For more details on examining these two documents, review "Monitoring of Current Status" in sessions 3, 5, and 6.)

Agenda Setting

You and your client will go over the ten-question self-assessment that he completed from the preview section of his manual. You will also ask him what he would like to share from the writing in his Therapy Journal. (For more information on examining the self-assessment and the Therapy Journal, review "Agenda Setting" in session 3.)

While setting the agenda this session, pay particular attention to the core beliefs that are grounded in the client's real-life events. Don't be surprised if he has some initial trouble recognizing them right away. When brought out into the light of day, the beliefs often seem exaggerated or extreme. If he remains unsure, suggest you and he try some work during session with a "tentative" core belief and see if there is any therapeutic progress to be made.

Specific goals for this session include:

1. Reviewing homework from session 8

2. Educating the client about core beliefs and exploring his core beliefs in-session

3. Exploring correlations between his personal relationships and core beliefs

Review of Homework from Session 8

How did the thought-stopping go? Did your client have fun with it? Did he let himself get into the yelling and jumping up and down? The more demonstrative he can be the better. Ruminative thinking needs something stronger than more thinking to really put a halt to it.

Notice the anxiety reactions reflected in the Worry Record and Thought Record. Did the client draw upon thought-stopping to deal with his anxiety? Make sure to discuss the results, whether favorable or not. If the client did not use thought-stopping you might inquire as to why not and look to the week's therapy records to see how this skill might have been applied.

If your client did not experience success, why not? Perhaps he was feeling too inhibited—not surprising for an anxious person. Perhaps he felt flooded by negative thoughts and couldn't identify specific ones on which to try thought-stopping. Review your therapy notes of the sessions so far to select strong automatic thoughts that have driven your client's anxiety. You may use these in session by taking on the negative thoughts and then using thought-stopping. Or perhaps the individual feels it's useless to try to affect the course of his thinking. This would suggest a depressive outlook, on this topic at least, and you would want to determine if a stronger depression may coexist with the anxiety. If so, treat as necessary. If there is not a separate depression, you can address these helpless and hopeless thoughts by engaging the client to challenge to what extent they are true as well as test the consequences of believing them.

Concepts and Skills

Psychoeducation

Core Beliefs

If CBT can be regarded as a psychology of belief, the furthest reach of that psychology would be in what is called the core beliefs. These are our deepest conceptions of what we assume to be true about ourselves and our world (particularly the people in it). Core beliefs combine what we feel emotionally, how we act, what we know, how we perceive the environment around us, and what we draw from our memory. They are deeply wrought by our experience, especially that which has been traumatic. As such, the core beliefs enact certain patterns that unfold over the course of our lives and serve to reinforce our belief in the truth of the core beliefs themselves. To a significant degree we are not aware of our core beliefs. They are so much a part of us it is difficult to gain the necessary perspective to see their independent existence. There seems to be a quality about many core beliefs that seeks to persuade us that they do not really exist.

Most core beliefs would remain quietly influential from the shadows of our minds were it not for disruptive events that bring them to the surface. It is these breaks of continuity in our lives that thrust the core beliefs into view. Your client is likely in the midst of such a disruption as evidenced by his development of GAD and his seeking treatment for its relief. Both the psychological condition itself and the treatment for it have a significant uncovering effect for the core beliefs. It is only logical, then, that this is the final main topic to be addressed before the close of therapy.

A number of therapists find core beliefs to be the most compelling part of CBT treatment. This can be seen as the heart and soul of the therapy. By this point you probably have a good sense of your client's core beliefs, particularly the ones that drive his anxiety. They have likely emerged in a variety of ways in your preceding sessions, and this is the opportunity to address them directly. Some clients can now realize that their spontaneous discussions in their Therapy Journal were actually their early grasp of their core beliefs. Should your client hit a blank when he first hears about core beliefs, it would be a good idea for you to have one close at hand that you and he have dealt with earlier in therapy. Once the pump is primed in this way, there is usually no problem finding and exploring the related core beliefs.

Skill Building

Exploring Core Beliefs during the Session

1. **Identify the Core Beliefs**

   As you and your client review his Thought Records that you asked him to bring in at the end of the last session, you and he will probably notice certain patterns about his worries. The same kinds of concerns typically keep surfacing over and over. Even as he makes headway with his therapy and reduces his anxiety, there are likely certain deeper beliefs that remain. Core beliefs are what he believes at the deepest level about himself and his world. They probably originated in his childhood and have gained strength since then. Core beliefs influence us to act in ways that reinforce the beliefs.

   He'll probably recognize a wide path where he has traveled in this therapy. He may want to share some of his reactions with you. These records provide an unusually good source for your client to really get his hands on his core beliefs. Ask him to write down the automatic thoughts and images that appear in his Thought Records, particularly when they cluster together in patterns.

   You can further help him uncover his core beliefs by teaching him to use a technique called the downward arrow to explore the deeper implications. In his therapy work so far he has probably found there are different degrees of truth to his thinking, depending on how realistic or anxious or depressed he may be at that time. For purposes of the downward arrow, he should assume that a given automatic thought is completely true and then follow the implications of that being so. For example, if such and such really is true, what does it mean?

2. **Assess the Negative Impact**

   Your client has a variety of core beliefs that are a healthy and fundamental part of him. They account for his individuality and his formative influences over the years. Healthy core beliefs might include his attitudes toward giving, his determination for hard work, his appreciation of a good time, or his self-acceptance (problems and all). There are many others.

   For the purposes of therapy we are more concerned about the negative core beliefs. These are the origins of the life patterns that makes your client and the people around him suffer unnecessarily. Over the course of this therapy he has probably become more aware of the varieties of suffering in his life, particularly that caused by anxiety. What are the broad consequences of this pain? How is his life troubled or diminished by his negative core beliefs that do not go away?

How might other people around him feel pain by reason of his core beliefs? And how does he feel pain on account of theirs?

3. Find the Underlying Rules

Every core belief is maintained by its own set of underlying rules. The rules evolve over time and are your client's observations about how life really works. Sometimes the rules are told to him, but more often he figures them out along the way. They are his best effort to avoid pain in his life and for the people around him.

Most often, he has only a shadowy view of what his rules really are. In day-to-day life they are never exactly looked at nor discussed in clear terms. In this session you want to help your client bring the rules out into the light of day so he can begin to determine which ones he wants to keep and which are ready to be retired.

Rules can usually be stated in the form of "If . . . then . . ." statements. For example, "If I speak up, then I will be criticized" or "If I ask for what I want, then I will make other people uncomfortable." These would be rules that support a core belief of "I'm not worthy."

4. Find the Consequences for Breaking the Rules

Rules are rules because they hold some power if they are broken. From your client's earliest experience as a child he learned there are consequences for breaking the rules. The same holds true in his adult life. He wants to figure out the enforcement or punishment for his rules. At first this might seem odd to him, but over time he'll begin to see what he imagines to be the negative consequences to breaking the rules. Most often the full punishment never happens because he has been compliant and not challenged the rules. And so they live on.

5. Select the Rules to Be Tested

Now it's time to begin challenging certain of the rules. Ask your client to pick one that is relatively low risk. There shouldn't be huge consequences riding on it. Help him try to figure a situation that tests the core belief directly with as few other influences as possible. He'll know he is on track if he can make a clear prediction of results—what would be the consequences that would challenge the validity of the rule and what results would support it. It's better if the conclusion is immediate or short-term, compared to something that would take a lot of time to unfold.

6. Test the Rules

Once he has identified a low-risk situation, ask him to predict the outcome of his acting contrary to the rule. Now the most important part will be determining exactly what alternate way he is going to act. He should carefully prepare himself, by planning his actions step by step, to give this experiment the best chance of working. Ask him to visualize the full set of actions with a positive outcome.

Testing Core Beliefs in Real Life

Your client will be practicing the above steps by himself at home by actually testing the rule in his real life. Find someone who supports him in this process. Tell him to ask for tough feedback from that person to make sure he is not sabotaging himself or omitting important success factors. When he's done, he should ask himself the following questions: What were the results? How did he feel during the test? Did he find new experiences contrary to the core belief? What were the negative consequences of challenging the old rule?

Next, your client can modify the test according to what he learned and broaden the situations where he applies it. He should gradually increase the risk factor he is willing to tolerate. Remind him that this kind of change is challenging and he'll need lots of support.

Finally, your client can begin revising his core beliefs according to his new experiences of himself and the world around him. These beliefs can include more of the positive results from his current life rather than just the negative history from his past. The revised beliefs are likely to be more flexible and include input from new learning (such as resulting from these experiments). He'll probably find less anxiety associated with these core beliefs. His revised rules should be more obvious to him and less shadowy. Consequences for challenging these rules will be less punitive.

Personal Relationships and Revising Core Beliefs

More than anything else, core beliefs originate in people's relations with other people. Your client will likely see ample evidence of core beliefs in whatever dealings he has with the people in his life. Even how your client relates to himself falls into the field of view for core beliefs. Is your client becoming aware of whom among his friends and loved ones trigger specific core beliefs in him? In which relationships does he feel free to move beyond the anxieties and the boundaries of his old core beliefs? Are there certain relationships in which he finds himself enacting his long-held beliefs, even when the other person is doing little to make that happen and wishes it were not so? This whole area may become a source of ongoing interest for your client and perhaps contribute to his personal growth after the therapy has come to an end.

Session Summary

Briefly summarize the material covered in the session. Try to reflect those learning points personally notable to your client. If your client disagrees with or seems to not understand your summary, you should ask him questions to find out why.

Feedback from Client

At the conclusion of each session, ask your client for feedback about the usefulness of the material and any questions that may remain. Encourage him to give feedback so that you can address any concerns that may have arisen.

Homework for This Session

1. Ask your client to try to make revisions in at least one of his core beliefs before the next session by completing steps 1 through 7 (in his manual) at least once. You'll want to help your client make a good start on revising the core beliefs that drive his anxiety. The therapy you have done so far has provided an important shift in that direction.

2. Ask your client to complete his third and final STAI, and bring it with him to his next session.

3. Remind him to complete his Daily Worry Record and Thought Record and bring the records with him to the next session.

4. Remind him to read the "Preview to Session 10" that appears in his manual. As discussed in session 2, he will need to complete the ten-question self-assessment that appears in that section of the manual and bring it with him to the next session with you.

5. You and your client are preparing to make next week the final session of your regular meetings. In preparation, this would be a good time to ask him to reread his Therapy Journal, Thought Records, and Daily Worry Records. You'll be discussing together with him the most significant parts of his therapy, so make sure to ask him to write down any remaining issues or questions that need to be addressed before the end of treatment.

6. Ask your client to complete the Program Satisfaction Questionnaire (found in the client manual) to help you both determine how successful the treatment has been.

Ready to Finish

Some clients are essentially finished with their GAD treatment at this time; they are basically comfortable with their current core beliefs. They're ready to stop their therapy after next week's session. This applies to approximately 70 percent of the clients who have reached this point in therapy.

Ready to Finish with a Booster

Other clients have made substantial progress in overcoming their anxiety and are prepared to continue the process of revising their core beliefs on their own, using the therapeutic methods described in this session. These clients are ready to stop regular therapy after next week's session, but could benefit from a booster session with you in approximately three months. If this applies to your client, he would work on his core beliefs with plans to touch base with you in three months. Meeting again is a nice way to reinforce his independent therapy work.

Need to Continue

A minority of clients may need to continue regular therapy with you beyond next week's session. Their gains in overcoming their anxiety may still be tentative or their core beliefs may still have a powerful effect in keeping their anxiety high. Continued sessions would focus on those particular therapy skills you and he consider to be most useful in decreasing the residual anxiety, and would target the specific core beliefs that are driving the anxiety. Naturally you and your client would collaborate in making these revised plans for the therapy and discuss regularly the status of his ongoing work.

For you and your client to decide when to finish therapy, you both can draw upon a variety of sources of clinical data. Your primary reference, of course, will be the client's self-report. How does he feel about his anxiety now? Has there been improvement in his day-to-day life? What is his feeling about how he'll do in the future? How do these reflections compare with your own experience of the individual? You'll draw upon your clinical judgment while sorting this through with your client to arrive at a consensus decision.

Your data sources will also include the final STAI, which you have asked him to complete between this session and next. This serves as a posttreatment measure of your client's anxiety. You would be looking for scores of S-anxiety and T-anxiety in the normal range. (For more information, see Appendix A.) Next session, you will check to see how these current scores compare with the client's measures at beginning of treatment and midtherapy. You will check for progress and take a look at what issues remain.

An additional source of information will be the client's completed therapy work from his manual. At this point you have a rich account of his week-by-week progress reflected in his Worry Records and Thought Records, as well as his Therapy Journal. As you and your client review this material, you both will likely recognize where there have been gains and what, if any, questions remain.

Session 10

Relapse Prevention

Monitoring of Current Status

Again, begin by asking the client whether any significant concerns—related to therapy or otherwise—have arisen since the previous session. Remember to try to keep this early discussion under ten minutes. (You may want to review "Monitoring of Current Status" in session 2.)

This is the last time you and your client will discuss her Worry Record and Thought Record. What do these documents reflect about the client's early stages of confronting her core beliefs? Were there changes in her levels of anxiety or perceived levels of threat? If so, you will explore with the client what happened and how this can be resolved. Do the records reflect the client's reactions to termination of therapy? For example, do you see evidence of anxiety that might be triggered by finishing the therapeutic relationship with you? Do you see the avoidance of anxiety about termination? Obviously these are important topics to discuss as you work out plans to terminate her therapy.

Agenda Setting

You and your client will go over the ten-question self-assessment that she completed from the preview section of her manual. You will also ask her what she would like to share from the writing in her Therapy Journal. (For more information on examining the self-assessment and the Therapy Journal, review "Agenda Setting" in session 3.)

In developing an agenda for this last session together, explore in detail whatever concerns your client may have about the conclusion of therapy. This is a common theme with termination, particularly following treatment of anxiety. Ask the client what her current worries are as well as what she anticipates they might be in the future. You will help guide your client in planning the therapeutic methods and outlook that will help her overcome these fears. If no particular concerns surface for your client, you might inquire about other endings in her life (such as relationships or employment) to determine if termination themes in those situations might apply here. Of course, your client could well feel positive about ending therapy after good gains; there may be no particular concerns. In that case, this session could be best used by reviewing what has been learned in this successful treatment.

Specific goals for this session include:

1. Reviewing homework from session 9

2. Educating the client about relapse prevention

3. Exploring correlations between her personal relationships and relapse prevention

Review of Homework from Session 9

Working with core beliefs usually generates strong emotional reactions. Bringing these deep patterns out into the open may engender relief, regret, hope, or sorrow. As your client is discussing the core beliefs that came to light, pay attention to her emotional experience as communicated to you. By this time you've worked with this individual for nearly two months and you likely have your own sense of her core beliefs and the associated feelings. How does her experience compare with your empathic reading of the same material? Do you feel closer to her during this discussion or do you feel pushed away? These reactions on your part are all clinical data that reflect how she relates to her core beliefs and what happens when she shares this experience with other people.

Was she able to make headway in challenging some of the rules of the old core beliefs? Did she find current life circumstances where she was able to test the predictions based upon those old beliefs? In reviewing this homework, you can point the client in the direction of further growth in revising core beliefs. Ask about the related beliefs that she wants to work on, and you can add those that you have recognized over the course of the work together. This work can be ongoing after the conclusion of therapy.

What are the core beliefs specifically linked to anxiety? Have there been beliefs related to experiencing the world as a threatening place? What about beliefs related to seeing oneself as lacking the skills and resources to deal with the threats at hand? Discuss with your client whether the therapy experiences have caused a revision in these beliefs. How can she respond to triggering situations that formerly triggered the old core beliefs associated with anxiety but now have a more positive outcome?

You'll be interpreting your client's final STAI results during this session. What do the results show about the progress she has made in therapy? How does she feel about the results?

Finally, what are the results of the Program Satisfaction Questionnaire? Does the client feel that the treatment was helpful? Why or why not?

Concepts and Skills

Psychoeducation

Relapse Prevention

CBT treatment of anxiety is based upon a recovery model rather than an aim for a complete cure. This acknowledges that because of a person's biological predisposition as well as cumulative life experience, there will be a tendency for an individual who has once had GAD to experience at least some anxiety in the years to come. The long-term effectiveness of this treatment rests upon whether your client can adequately deal with those future anxiety triggers so she can avert a new episode of GAD or whether her condition deteriorates to a full relapse. The gains of a successful treatment for GAD need to be consolidated in such a way that they can be effectively used by your client in the future. This is why, as a key part of drawing this therapy to a close, you will help your client prepare to apply these therapeutic lessons when she is on her own.

You will be reviewing with your client what have been the most effective methods for her recovery from anxiety. It is helpful in advance for you to have prepared your thoughts on the matter since you may have a broader scope and more complete memory of this than the client. You and your client will also consider her end-of-treatment STAI, so you should have her earlier scores handy. Finally, review any unresolved emotional or personal issues in the therapy so these can be discussed and settled.

Skill Building

In-Session Preparation for Relapse Prevention

1. **Review the Methods That Worked**

   It is a good idea for the client to review the methods that have worked for her. In all likelihood, some were more helpful to her than others. You and your client probably modified certain features for the best fit in her situation. Ask her to make a list of the therapy skills she's learned and evaluate to what extent they helped her. She should include ways in which she changed them to make a better fit for herself. As your client generates this list in session, do you see any methods that have been useful to her that she has overlooked? You can fill in what is missing.

2. **Maintain Positive Therapy Directions**

   Ask her to consider the life changes she's made over the course of her therapy and how they led to overcoming her anxiety. This would be an important time for her to make a commitment to building those same activities into her ongoing life. Why give them up now? Didn't they lead to positive life experiences? Notice whether your client's stated level of commitment to change really fits with the emotional tone of how she expresses herself. If you are aware of some level of anxiety, gently offer this observation. The client may mistakenly think that to make a positive future for herself she needs to leave behind all anxiety. By your modeling a balanced approach in this final session you are leaving a lasting example that hope and a little anxiety about the future can coexist.

3. **Remain Aware of Unfinished Issues**

    Even with a successful therapy, there are issues that are not completely resolved. There is not time nor opportunity to take care of everything at once. For your client it might be unsettled feelings about the breakup of a relationship, continuing conflict with a neighbor, or remaining doubts whether she can make it on her own after therapy. You and your client will likely recognize those topics that, though working on them has led to progress, have not been fully concluded yet.

4. **Identify Triggers and Early Warning Signs**

    Your client's long-term freedom from GAD depends upon knowing what could readily activate her anxiety in the future. Upon finishing her therapy she is ideally situated to recognize her potential triggers and how they could be handled so they don't get out of hand. Remaining aware of her early warning signs is the best way for her to make prompt response so that circumstances do not escalate to another episode of GAD. As an additional means of bringing this step to life, you might review how early warning signs have emerged over the course of the sessions.

Out-of-Session Relapse Prevention

In addition to putting the above steps into action on a regular basis, your client should be made aware of the following two guidelines:

1. **Friends Who Keep Your Client Honest**

    It's easy for your client to get wrapped up in her life and perhaps not even notice if she's drifting back into anxiety. Anxiety tends to reduce awareness so that it can slip back silently. That's why it's vital to have certain friends and loved ones with whom she keeps close contact so they can see how she is really doing, beneath the surface. It's ideal if they've also been the ones who supported her through this therapy process and talked with her about what she has learned. Tell her to keep in touch with these people and let them know that she welcomes their honest opinions about how she is doing. She should listen carefully if they have concerns, and she should offer the same kind of constructive feedback to them in how they are living their lives.

2. **A Monthly STAI**

    Ask your client to consider taking a monthly STAI. Only fifteen minutes a month are required to get a quick reading of how she feels and whether her anxiety has been reactivated. She could compare those future scores with how she feels now, at the end of therapy. Tell her to think of it as a doctor's follow-up after she's been successfully treated for a physical condition.

Personal Relationships and Relapse Prevention

The single best predictor of continued success in freedom from anxiety is the quality of your client's ongoing personal relationships. To the extent that she enjoys strong and reciprocal relationships, she will be optimally suited to manage anxiety triggers that may arise. Over the course of therapy you and your client have likely recognized those relationships in her life that have reinforced her growth in overcoming anxiety. At the same time you probably also examined those features of relationships that have tended to promote her anxiety. It might be those people who are threatening or unpredictable toward her, or those who are overly protective and worrisome, or those who fail to take responsibility for themselves and depend upon the client excessively. For there to have been significant gains for your client in dealing with her anxiety, there likely have also occurred collateral improvements in these kinds of relationships. The client is now better able to voice what is favorable in a relationship and what needs to change. She can stand up for the principles of how she wants to be treated and how she treats others. And, if the other person refuses to alter his or her anxiety-toxic behaviors, the client can step back and decrease the psychological influence of that individual.

These insights about personal relationships as derived over the course of therapy will likely be reviewed between you and your client as you prepare to draw the therapy to a close. You may also want to acknowledge what has felt meaningful about the therapeutic relationship that has contributed to your client's success in overcoming anxiety. After all, more than anything else it has been the therapeutic relationship between you and your client that has accounted for these therapeutic gains.

Session Summary

Briefly summarize the material covered in the session. Try to reflect those learning points personally notable to your client. If your client disagrees with or seems to not understand your summary, you should ask her questions to find out why.

Feedback from Client

At the conclusion of each session, ask your client for feedback about the usefulness of the material and any questions that may remain. Encourage her to give feedback so that you can address any concerns that may have arisen. Explore in detail her responses to the Program Satisfaction Questionnaire that appears in her client manual. Use this as an opportunity to learn what about this treatment approach worked and what didn't. How can you make future adjustments?

This will be the final session with your client. You should discuss with her her feelings about the therapy process as a whole. Does she have any concerns about the termination? Remind her of how the plan you and she developed will help prevent a relapse of GAD. In addition, keeping in mind the nature of the collaborative relationship, it is appropriate to consider sharing your feelings about the therapy and what it has meant for you to work with this client. This disclosure on your part will be determined by what is in the best interest of the client.

Arranging Follow-up

In drawing this therapy to a close, you may choose to make yourself available for future work with the client should the need arise. Not only is this usually viewed as a reassuring message to the client, but it lends itself to a good model for CBT therapy. Nicholas

Cummings (1995) has called this "brief, intermittent therapy over the lifespan." A client who has benefited from treatment of GAD will probably encounter certain anxiety issues in the future. With brief focused work provided by a familiar therapist who draws upon the success of earlier treatment, most new issues can be quickly resolved. There need be no relapse of GAD.

Appendix 1

The STAI

Introduction to the STAI

The STAI was standardized and validated on more than twelve hundred high school and college students; eighteen hundred working adults; fifteen hundred military recruits; six hundred neuropsychiatric, medical, and surgical patients; and two hundred prison inmates (Okun et al. 1996). It was reliable and internally consistent (the alpha ranged from .86 to .95). Scores correlated with expected results under stressful and non-stressful experimental conditions and discriminated neuropsychiatric patients from community residents (Spielberger 1983).

Using the STAI

The first step in the therapeutic process is for you and your client to determine whether there is truly a diagnosis of GAD. At the beginning of therapy (session 1) you undertake a detailed assessment of your client so you both can understand the origins and present manifestation of her anxiety. If there is sufficient evidence of GAD to continue onward with therapy, between sessions 1 and 2 you will ask her to complete the STAI. You might describe the rationale as follows or find your own way to explain it. "This test will help us get another view of your anxiety. We can compare your results with people who are your gender and age. This lets us measure your anxiety to better determine what you want to change and to assess our progress in ongoing therapy. It's like a second opinion that adds to what we have learned so far. There are no right or wrong answers; just respond with your first impression that seems to best apply to you. Don't think too long or too hard about it. Of course the results will be completely confidential just like everything else we discuss in therapy. Any questions?" The test usually takes between six and ten minutes to complete. Have the client bring the results to the next session with you.

Self-Evaluation Questionnaire
STAI Form Y-1

Please provide the following information:

Name _____ Date _____ S ____

Age _____ Gender (Circle) M   F   T ____

Directions:

A number of statements which people have used to describe themselves are given below. Read each statement and then circle the appropriate number to the right of the statement to indicate how you feel *right* now, that is, *at this moment*. There are no right or wrong answers. Do not spend too much time on any one statement but give the answer which seems to describe your present feelings best.

	Not At All	Somewhat	Moderately So	Very Much So
1. I feel calm	1	2	3	4
2. I feel secure	1	2	3	4
3. I feel tense	1	2	3	4
4. I feel strained	1	2	3	4
5. I feel at ease	1	2	3	4
6. I feel upset	1	2	3	4
7. I am presently worrying over possible misfortunes	1	2	3	4
8. I feel satisfied	1	2	3	4
9. I feel frightened	1	2	3	4
10. I feel comfortable	1	2	3	4
11. I feel self-confident	1	2	3	4
12. I feel nervous	1	2	3	4
13. I am jittery	1	2	3	4
14. I feel indecisive	1	2	3	4
15. I am relaxed	1	2	3	4
16. I feel content	1	2	3	4
17. I am worried	1	2	3	4
18. I feel confused	1	2	3	4
19. I feel steady	1	2	3	4
20. I feel pleasant	1	2	3	4

Used with permission of Mind Garden™, and is available from fax: (650) 261-3505 or email: info@mindgarden.com

Self-Evaluation Questionnaire
STAI Form Y-2

Please provide the following information:

Name _____ Date _____ S ____

Age _____ Gender (Circle) M   F   T ____

Directions:

A number of statements which people have used to describe themselves are given below. Read each statement and then circle the appropriate number to the right of the statement to indicate how you *generally* feel.

	Almost Never	Sometimes	Often	Almost Always
21. I feel pleasant	1	2	3	4
22. I feel nervous and restless	1	2	3	4
23. I feel satisfied with myself	1	2	3	4
24. I wish I could be as happy as others seem to be	1	2	3	4
25. I feel like a failure	1	2	3	4
26. I feel rested	1	2	3	4
27. I am "calm, cool, and collected"	1	2	3	4
28. I feel that difficulties are piling up so that I cannot overcome them	1	2	3	4
29. I worry too much over something that really doesn't matter	1	2	3	4
30. I am happy	1	2	3	4
31. I have disturbing thoughts	1	2	3	4
32. I lack self-confidence	1	2	3	4
33. I feel secure	1	2	3	4
34. I make decisions easily	1	2	3	4
35. I feel inadequate	1	2	3	4
36. I am content	1	2	3	4
37. Some unimportant thought runs through my mind and bothers me	1	2	3	4
38. I take disappointments so keenly that I can't put them out of my mind	1	2	3	4
39. I am a steady person	1	2	3	4
40. I get in a state of tension or turmoil as I think over my recent concerns and interests	1	2	3	4

State-Trait Anxiety Inventory for Adults Scoring Key

To use this stencil, fold this sheet in half and line up with the appropriate test side, either Form Y-1 or Form Y-2. Simply total the scoring **weights** shown on the stencil for each response category. For example, for question #1, if the respondent marked 3, then the **weight** would be **2**. Refer to the manual for appropriate normative data.

Form Y-1	Not At All	Somewhat	Moderately So	Very Much So		Form Y-2	Almost Never	Sometimes	Often	Almost Always
1.	4	3	2	1		21.	4	3	2	1
2.	4	3	2	1		22.	1	2	3	4
3.	1	2	3	4		23.	4	3	2	1
4.	1	2	3	4		24.	1	2	3	4
5.	4	3	2	1		25.	1	2	3	4
6.	1	2	3	4		26.	4	3	2	1
7.	1	2	3	4		27.	4	3	2	1
8.	4	3	2	1		28.	1	2	3	4
9.	1	2	3	4		29.	1	2	3	4
10.	4	3	2	1		30.	4	3	2	1
11.	4	3	2	1		31	1	2	3	4
12.	1	2	3	4		32.	1	2	3	4
13.	1	2	3	4		33.	4	3	2	1
14.	1	2	3	4		34.	4	3	2	1
15.	4	3	2	1		35.	1	2	3	4
16.	4	3	2	1		36.	4	3	2	1
17.	1	2	3	4		37.	1	2	3	4
18.	1	2	3	4		38.	1	2	3	4
19.	4	3	2	1		39.	4	3	2	1
20.	4	3	2	1		40.	1	2	3	4

Scoring the STAI

Items 1 through 20 measure what Spielberger calls S-anxiety. This is the immediate anxiety your client experiences at the present time of taking the test. You will notice that each STAI item is given a weighted score of 1 to 4. A rating of 4 indicates the presence of a high level of anxiety for ten S-anxiety items. Refer to #3 "I feel tense" and #4 "I feel strained." By contrast, the remaining ten S-anxiety items are reversed so that 4 indicates the absence of anxiety, as seen in #1 "I feel calm" and #2 "I feel secure." The scoring weights for the anxiety-present items are the same as the blackened numbers of the test form. *The scoring weights for the anxiety-absent items are reversed, that is, responses marked 1, 2, 3, or 4 are scored 4, 3, 2, or 1, respectively.* The anxiety-absent items for which the scoring weights are reversed on the S-anxiety scale are:

S-anxiety: 1, 2, 5, 8, 10, 11, 15, 16, 19, 20

To obtain a raw score for the S-anxiety scale, simply add the weighted scores for the twenty items that make up each scale, taking into account the fact that the scores are reversed for the above items. Scores can vary from a minimum of 20 to a maximum of 80.

Items 21 through 40 measure T-anxiety, the individual's general tendency toward anxiety. As above, a rating of 4 indicates the presence of a high level of anxiety for eleven T-anxiety items, such as #22 "I feel nervous and restless" and #24 "I wish I could be as happy as others seem to be." By contrast the remaining nine T-anxiety items are reversed, as seen in #21 "I feel pleasant" and #23 "I feel satisfied with myself." *Remember to reverse the scoring weights for the anxiety-absent items:*

T-anxiety: 21, 23, 26, 27, 30, 33, 34, 36, 39

You will calculate the T-anxiety scale in the same manner by adding the weighted scores for the twenty items that make up each scale, taking into account the reversed items. Scores can range for 20 to 80.

Applying STAI Norms

Your calculations have created a raw score for both S-anxiety and T-anxiety. Using the appropriate gender and age norms tables for your client, translate these new scores to percentiles. For example, a thirty-one-year-old female with an S-anxiety raw score of thirty-nine would translate to a percentile of seventy-one. Her T-anxiety raw score of thirty-five would translate to a percentile of fifty-four. This means that compared to the general population her immediate stress (S-anxiety) would measure greater than 70 percent of people. Her anxious outlook (T-anxiety) would measure greater than 53 percent of people.

Percentile Ranks for Normal Adults
in Three Age Groups

Raw Score	19–39				40–49				50–69				Raw Score
	Males		Females		Males		Females		Males		Females		
	State	Trait	State	Trait	State	Trait	State	Trait	State	Trait	State	Trait	
80	100	100	100	100	100	100	100	100	100	100	100	100	80
79	100	100	100	100	100	100	100	100	100	100	100	100	79
78	100	100	100	100	100	100	100	100	100	100	100	100	78
77	100	100	100	100	100	100	100	100	100	100	100	100	77
76	100	100	100	100	100	100	100	100	100	100	100	100	76
75	100	100	100	100	100	100	100	100	100	100	100	100	75
74	100	100	100	100	100	100	100	100	100	100	100	100	74
73	100	100	100	100	100	100	100	100	100	100	100	100	73
72	100	100	100	100	100	100	100	100	100	100	100	100	72
71	100	100	100	100	100	100	100	100	100	100	100	100	71
70	100	100	100	100	100	100	100	100	100	100	100	100	70
69	100	100	100	100	100	100	100	100	100	100	100	100	69
68	100	100	100	100	100	100	100	100	100	100	100	100	68
67	100	100	100	100	99	100	100	100	100	100	100	100	67
66	100	100	99	100	99	100	99	100	100	100	100	100	66
65	100	100	99	100	98	100	99	100	100	100	99	100	65
64	100	100	88	100	98	100	99	100	99	100	99	100	64
63	100	100	98	100	98	100	98	100	99	100	99	100	63
62	99	100	97	100	98	100	96	99	99	100	99	100	62
61	98	99	95	99	98	100	96	99	99	100	99	100	61
60	98	99	95	98	98	100	96	99	98	100	99	100	60
59	98	98	95	97	97	100	96	99	98	100	99	100	59
58	97	98	95	96	96	99	96	99	97	100	99	100	58
57	96	98	94	95	96	99	94	99	97	99	99	100	57
56	95	97	94	95	95	99	94	97	96	98	99	100	56
55	94	96	93	95	94	98	93	96	96	98	99	100	55
54	94	96	92	94	94	97	93	95	96	98	99	100	54
53	93	95	91	93	93	97	93	94	95	97	99	99	53
52	92	94	91	93	93	96	91	93	94	96	99	99	52
51	91	94	89	93	92	94	89	92	94	96	99	99	51
50	90	92	89	92	90	93	87	92	92	94	99	98	50
49	88	90	87	92	89	92	87	92	91	94	97	97	49
48	86	88	85	90	88	90	87	90	89	93	97	97	48
47	85	87	84	89	87	89	85	89	87	92	93	97	47
46	82	85	82	86	85	87	82	87	85	91	93	97	46
45	80	83	81	86	83	86	81	87	84	90	93	96	45
44	78	81	79	83	81	84	78	84	83	88	93	95	44
43	76	78	77	80	78	82	75	82	81	86	90	93	43
42	73	76	76	76	76	81	74	80	79	84	87	92	42
41	70	74	73	72	72	78	72	78	76	81	85	88	41
40	66	71	71	69	70	76	67	78	74	77	82	84	40

Raw Score	19–39				40–49				50–69				Raw Score
	Males		Females		Males		Females		Males		Females		
	State	Trait	State	Trait	State	Trait	State	Trait	State	Trait	State	Trait	
39	64	69	71	66	67	73	67	74	72	74	80	83	39
38	61	66	68	65	64	68	67	70	69	71	76	81	38
37	58	63	62	61	62	65	64	65	66	68	74	76	37
36	55	59	59	59	58	62	58	63	64	63	72	73	36
35	50	57	56	54	56	60	55	57	60	61	69	69	35
34	46	52	52	50	53	54	53	53	55	59	66	66	34
33	44	48	48	47	48	49	50	50	52	55	61	59	33
32	39	43	44	42	43	44	49	45	48	49	59	56	32
31	36	38	41	35	39	39	43	44	45	45	51	51	31
30	31	33	40	29	35	34	39	37	40	39	47	44	30
29	28	30	34	25	27	28	33	33	36	36	37	39	29
28	25	27	30	22	24	24	24	27	33	31	35	34	28
27	19	24	21	18	22	21	22	22	28	27	32	31	27
26	16	21	17	16	19	18	19	17	26	24	31	30	26
25	14	15	13	12	16	14	16	14	21	19	28	27	25
24	12	12	10	9	14	11	16	11	18	15	24	23	24
23	9	11	9	7	12	8	13	7	16	11	22	19	23
22	8	7	6	3	9	5	8	5	11	8	12	14	22
21	6	4	3	3	6	3	5	2	9	6	8	8	21
20	4	3	2	0	5	1	3	0	6	3	5	7	20

Interpreting the STAI

When Spielberger refers to "state anxiety" he means an individual's stress level at a particular moment. To keep this simple for your client, think of state anxiety as her level of immediate stress. It is typically your client's first reaction to a current situation that carries some threat or uncertainty for her. For example, an individual's perception of stress typically increases when facing surgery, going to the dentist, interviewing for a job, or taking an important school test. When these stressors are over with and settled, the individual's sense of immediate stress usually goes down.

When your client's sense of her own stress is low (below the fiftieth percentile S-anxiety), she usually has a feeling of being calm and serene. Whatever kinds of risk or uncertainty may exist in her life are not of particular concern at the present time. In the **mild range** of anxiety (fiftieth to sixty-fifth percentile S-anxiety), there are transient concerns but the individual is able to return to a relaxed state when the issues are over. In the **moderate range** (sixty-fifth to ninetieth percentile S-anxiety), your client probably experiences some tension and worry. There are usually issues that cause her to feel apprehensive and she is not sure how things will work out. High stress as measured on the STAI (above the ninetieth percentile S-anxiety) is the **severe range** and means that your client is likely experiencing intense fear, approaching terror or panic. She feels herself to be in a true crisis and, naturally, this will be your immediate focus in therapy. You will evaluate the nature of the risks your client is experiencing, assess the scope of her terrified reactions, and determine what means are necessary for crisis intervention.

Trait anxiety, on the other hand, is an ongoing tendency toward anxiety over the course of a lifetime. I will refer to this as an anxious outlook. This is an enduring life pattern in which a person has likely experienced significant anxiety in her past and expects more of the same in her future. In its purest sense this outlook is the individual's attempt to be as safe as possible by remaining on guard for all the things that could go wrong. A person doesn't simply decide to take on an anxious outlook—it runs deeper than a mere rational choice. It is no less powerful than an instinct to survive. Once the anxious outlook is deeply ingrained, there is an abiding tendency for it to continue onward regardless of life circumstance (even when life may be good, and self and loved ones are reasonably safe). Unfortunately, the longer one upholds an anxious outlook, the more likely that people and circumstances will come along to prove it true. If one is intent upon finding anxiety, there will probably be plenty of things to feel anxious about. The fact that there is almost always some basis in reality as to the sources of anxiety in the past makes the self-fulfilling prophesy of the anxious outlook all the stronger.

An individual can show tendency in the **mild range** toward an anxious outlook (fiftieth to sixty-fifth percentile T-anxiety) without presenting GAD (Trent et al. 1995). The anxiety is perceived as not getting out of hand nor showing destructive consequences to health or adjustment. In the **moderate range** of anxious outlook (sixty-fifth to ninetieth percentile T-anxiety) an individual is likely identifying the anxiety as a problem (Anderson, Noyes, and Crowe 1984). It may be interfering with work, relationships, health, or happiness. At this level the anxiety is felt to be a constant in the individual's life and probably warrants a diagnosis of GAD (Barlow, Rapee, and Brown 1992). In the **severe range** of anxious outlook (above the ninetieth percentile T-anxiety), the individual's life is dominated by anxiety (Roemer et al. 1995). She feels under constant threat and experiences insufficient personal resources to deal with the challenges. At this level of anxiety, a diagnosis of GAD is almost certainly warranted (Stanley, Beck, and Zebb 1996).

Does the stability of anxious outlook mean there is no changing it, that one is doomed to live this way for the rest of time? Not at all. But if there is to be change, it requires methods as strong as the anxiety. This is what therapy is all about. You and your client are working hard to make room for an outlook to life that is not based upon anxiety. She will explore the idea that not all worry is bad (session 2). Her practice with relaxation (session 3) gives her body a chance to feel calm rather than chronically tense. By means of risk assessment (session 4) she can validate the situations in which she is legitimately experiencing threat and, with problem solving (session 5), she can deal with it more effectively, She can gain confidence confronting the accumulated images that drive her anxiety (session 6) while stopping the behaviors (session 7) and thoughts (session 8) that needlessly put her back in the anxiety cycle. Having made this headway so far in therapy, she is prepared to dig down to the underlying beliefs (session 9) that originated the anxious outlook in the first place. And in concluding the work together you and she make plans how to hold onto the gains she has made (session 10) after therapy is over.

In using the STAI as a measure for treatment outcome, you will first ask your client to take it at the beginning of therapy. This will contribute to the diagnostic process and help set goals for therapy. The anxious outlook usually measures 65 percent or above for GAD clients, though the face-to-face interview is the ultimate measure of determining a diagnosis. A general goal for this type of GAD therapy is to reduce the anxious outlook to below 65 percent, lower if possible. In cases of extreme anxiety (90 percent and above), complete reduction below 65 percent may be a challenge, but client and therapist should expect at least a reduction of eight to ten points on the raw scores.

If an individual has a high immediate-stress rating but a relatively low anxious-outlook rating, consider whether she is experiencing situational problems rather than GAD. In such cases immediate stressors can be identified as well as a baseline before the crises that is relatively calm. You might consider crisis intervention and restabilization of resources, and the individual will probably respond quickly. If the anxiety persists, you might want to reevaluate the diagnosis and consider whether this treatment for GAD would be warranted.

You will repeat the STAI between sessions 5 and 6 for a measure of anxiety at the midpoint of therapy. Hopefully, you and your client will see improvements in both immediate stress and anxious outlook. This would be a good time to identify remaining issues of anxiety and discuss how to address them in the remaining sessions of therapy.

The final STAI will be taken between sessions 9 and 10. This will be part of the information that you and your client review as therapy is ending. Did his scores reflect significant improvement—beneath 65 percent T-anxiety or a decrease of a standard deviation (eight ot ten points)? At this time you and your client can discuss how to hold these gains as part of relapse prevention. If the scores show some remaining problems with anxiety, you can jointly address how best to deal with them.

Appendix 2

Top Ten Myths and Misconceptions about CBT

Perhaps you've encountered some of the myths or misconceptions about CBT. The ones I've heard are laid out here in a top-ten list. Since you may find the opportunity to address some of these issues with your clients or colleagues, brief responses are provided. At this point in your work with this treatment method, you ought to be able to give some pretty strong answers of your own.

CBT is a therapy characterized by ...

No feelings

There's plenty of emotional content. After all, how can you have strong thoughts without also having strong feelings?

No therapeutic relationship

It's called a collaborative relationship. The therapist is open, direct, cooperative, and—most importantly—empathic.

No history

How could this be so? Our deepest beliefs and life patterns derive from our history, right?

No real personality change

Sure, there can be significant change, but it starts sooner rather than later and comes in small doses during everyday life.

No depth

Wrong. CBT addresses profound matters of deep ambivalence and conflict. There are few easy answers.

For smart people only

This is probably the most inaccurate myth of all. CBT draws upon a commonsense approach, accessible at all intellectual levels.

A rigid approach

Each client sets individual goals for treatment and determines his or her own pace. There are no fixed theories about what everyone's psychology looks like.

A manual is a cookie cutter approach that treats all people alike

The manual draws together the best established practices for treating GAD. Each person learns and applies these tools in his or her own way.

Clients will hate the manual

On the contrary. Clients really appreciate having something tangible to hold on to that further links their day-to-day therapeutic work with you.

Selling out to managed care

CBT started well before managed care. Think of it as extra leverage to push back against insurance companies to better justify the care we provide.

Appendix 3

Treatment Plan

Problem: Excessive anxiety for a period of six months or longer.

Definition: Apprehension, tension, or uneasiness that stems from the anticipation of danger, which may be internal or external.

Goals: Reduce motor tension, autonomic hyperactivity, and vigilance and scanning.

Objectives	Interventions
1. Develop skills to focus anxiety.	Schedule worry time dedicated to a worthwhile topic of client's choosing.
2. Increase capacity for physical relaxation.	Relaxation in daily practice lowers physical stress level and targets anxiety triggers.
3. Generate accurate appraisal of threat.	Risk assessment analyzes threat and other outcomes plus client's resources to respond.
4. Make constructive solutions to problems.	Problem solving structures a process to undertake adaptation and evaluate results.
5. Decrease anxiety reactions to anxiety situations.	Worry exposure to desensitize client to hierarchy of stress images and situations.
6. Reduce safety behaviors that promote avoidance.	Reducing safety behaviors keeps the client from further avoiding triggers.
7. Stop repetitive thoughts associated with anxiety.	Thought-stopping for anxious ideation while moving client to preferred state of mind.

| 8. Revise the core beliefs that drive the anxiety cycle. | Revising core beliefs by testing old rules and amending to fit with contemporary life. |
| 9. Make plans to prevent a relapse of GAD. | Relapse prevention to generate a plan to deal with anxiety patterns and risks. |

Diagnosis: 300.02 Generalized Anxiety Disorder

Works Cited

American Psychiatric Association. 1994. *Diagnostic and statistical manual of mental disorders (DSM-IV)*. 4th ed. Washington, D.C.

Anderson, D. J., R. Noyes, and R. R. Crowe. 1984. A comparison of panic disorder and generalized anxiety disorder. *American Journal of Psychiatry* 141: 572–575.

Barlow, D. H. 1988. *Anxiety and its disorders*. New York: Guilford Press.

Barlow, D. H. 1993. Generalized anxiety disorder. In *Clinical handbook of psychological disorders*. 2d ed. New York: The Guilford Press.

Barlow, D. H., R. M. Rapee, and T. A. Brown. 1992. Behavioral treatment of generalized anxiety disorder. *Behavior Therapy* 23:551–570.

Beck, J. S. 1995. *Cognitive therapy*. New York: The Guilford Press.

Beck, A. T., and G. Emery. 1985. *Anxiety disorders and phobias*. New York: Basic Books.

Blowers, D., J. Cobb, and A. Matthews. 1987. Generalized anxiety. *Behavior Research and Therapy* 25:493–502.

Borkovec, T. D., A. M. Matthews, A. Chambers, S. Ebrahimi, R. Lytle, and R. Nelson. 1987. The effects of relaxation training with cognitive therapy or nondirective therapy and the role of relaxation-induced anxiety in the treatment of generalized anxiety. *Journal of Consulting and Clinical Psychology* 55:883–888.

Bourne, E. J. 1995. *The anxiety and phobia workbook*. 2d ed. Oakland: New Harbinger Publications.

Brown, T. A., R. M. Hertz, and D. H. Barlow. 1992. New developments in cognitive behavioral treatment of anxiety disorders. *American Psychiatric Press Review of Psychiatry* 11:285–306.

Butler, G., M. Fennell, D. Robson, and M. Gelder. 1991. Comparison of behavior therapy and cognitive-behavior therapy in the treatment of generalized anxiety disorder. *Journal of Consulting and Clinical Psychology* 59:167–175.

Clark, D. M. 1989. Anxiety states: Panic and generalized anxiety. In *Cognitive-behavior therapy for psychiatric problems: A practical guide*, edited by K. Hawton, P. M. Salkovskis, J. Kirk, and D. M. Clark. New York: Oxford University Press. 52–96.

Craske, M. G., R. M. Rapee, L. Jackel, and D. H. Barlow. 1989. Qualitative dimensions of worry in DSM-III-R generalized anxiety disorder subjects and nonanxious controls. *Behavior Research and Therapy* 27:397–402.

Craske, M. G., D. H. Barlow, and T. A. O'Leary. 1992. *Mastery of your anxiety and worry.* San Antonio: Graywind Publications.

Cummings, Nick. *Focused Psychotherapy.* 1995. New York: Brunner/Mazel.

D'Zurilla, T. J., and M. R. Goldfried. 1971. Problem solving and behavior modification. *Journal of Abnormal Psychology* 78: 107–126.

Ekman, P., and R. Davidson, eds. 1994. *Fundamental questions about emotions.* New York: Oxford University Press.

Foa, E. B., and M. J. Kozak. 1986. Emotional processing of fear. *Psychological Bulletin* 50:251–256.

Goleman, D. 1995. *Emotional intelligence.* New York: Bantam.

Hallowell, E. M. 1997. *Worry.* New York: Pantheon Books.

Hollon, S. D., and A. T. Beck. 1993. Cognitive and cognitive-behavioral therapies. In *Handbook of psychotherapy and behavior change.* 4th ed., edited by A.E. Bergin and S.L. Garfield. New York: Wiley. 428–466.

Kagan, J., N. Snidman, D. Arcus, and J. S. Reznick. 1997. *Galen's prophesy.* New York: Basic Books.

Lang, P. J. 1985. The cognitive psychophysiology of emotion. In *Anxiety and the anxiety disorders,* edited by A.H. Tuma and J. Maser. Hillsdale, N.J.: Erlbaum. 131–170.

Lindsay, W. R., C. V Gamsu, E. McLaughlin, E. M. Hood, and C. A. Espie. 1987. A controlled trial of treatments for generalized anxiety. *British Journal of Clinical Psychology* 26:3–15.

McKay, M., P. Fanning, and M. Davis. 1997. *Thoughts and feelings.* Oakland: New Harbinger Publications.

Okun, A., R. E. Stein, L. S. Bauman, and E. J. Silver. 1996. Content validity of the psychiatric symptom index, CES-depression scale, and state-trait anxiety inventory from the perspective of DSM-IV. *Psychological Reports* 79:1059–1069.

Padesky, C. A., and D. Greenberger. 1995. *Clinician's guide to mind over mood.* New York: Guilford Publications.

Persons, J. B. 1989. *Cognitive therapy in practice.* New York: W. W. Norton.

Roemer, E., and T. Borkovec. 1993. Worry. In *Handbook of mental control.* Vol. 5. Englewood Cliffs, N.J.: Prentice-Hall.

Roemer, E., M. Borkobec, S. Posa, and T. Borkovec. 1995. A self-report diagnostic measure of generalized anxiety disorder. *Journal of Behavior Therapy and Experimental Psychiatry* 26:345–350.

Slawsky, R. 1997. Personal communication.

Seligman, M. E. 1991. *Learned optimism.* New York: A. A. Knopf.

Spielberger, C. D. 1983. *State-trait anxiety inventory.* Palo Alto, Calif.: Mind Garden.

Spielberger, C. D. 1989. *State-trait anxiety inventory.* 2d ed. Palo Alto, Calif.: Consulting Psychologists Press.

Stanley, M. A., J. G. Beck, and B. J. Zebb. 1996. Psychometric properties and anxiety measures in older adults. *Behavior Research and Therapy* 34:827–838.

Trent, N. H., D. I. Templer, R. Gandolfo, M. Corgiat, and A. P. Trent. 1995. Multivariate investigation of anxiety in a psychiatric population. *Journal of Clinical Psychology* 51: 196–201.

Young, J. E. 1990. *Cognitive therapy for personality disorders.* Sarasota, Fla.: Professional Resources Exchange.

Zinbarg, R. E., D. H. Barlow, T. A. Brown, and R. M. Hertz. 1992. Cognitive-behavioral approaches to the nature and treatment of anxiety disorders. *Annual Review of Psychology* 43:235–267.

Suggested Reading

Books for People with GAD

Beck, A. T. *Love Is Never Enough*. New York: Harper and Row, 1988.

Benson, H. *The Relaxation Response*. New York: Morrow, 1975.

Bourne, E. J. *The Anxiety and Phobia Workbook*. 2d ed. Oakland, Calif.: New Harbinger Publications, 1995.

Burns, D. D. *The Feeling Good Handbook*. New York: Plume, 1989.

Greenberger, D., and C. Padesky. *Mind over Mood*. New York: Guilford Press, 1995.

Hallowell, E. M. *Worry*. New York: Random House, 1997.

Kabat-Zinn, J. *Full Catastrophe Living*. New York: Delacorte Press, 1990.

McKay, M., M. Davis, and P. Fanning. *Thoughts and Feelings*. Oakland, Calif.: New Harbinger Publications, 1997.

Seligman, M. E. P. *Learned Optimism*. New York: Simon and Schuster, 1990.

Young, J. E., and J. S. Klosko. *Reinventing Your Life*. New York: Dutton, 1993.

Relaxation Tapes

Guided Body Scan Meditation (two tapes)
   Jon Kabat-Zinn, Ph.D.
   Stress Reduction Tapes, P.O. Box 547, Lexington, MA 02173

Letting Go of Stress (one tape)
   Emmett Miller, M.D.
   Source, P.O. Box W, Stanford, CA 94305

Relaxation Training Program (three tapes)
   Thomas Budzynski, Ph.D.
   Guilford Publications, 72 Spring Street, New York, NY 10012

About the Author

John R. White, Ph.D., is the author of *Overcoming Generalized Anxiety Disorder*, an empirically based CBT treatment protocol published by New Harbinger. He is also an editor with Art Freeman, Ed.D. of *Cognitive Behavioral Group Therapies* to be published by APA Books in 2000. As Adjunct Professor at the California School of Professional Psychology-Alameda he teaches the Advanced Clinical Series in CBT and serves as Consulting Assistant Professor at Stanford University, School of Education for Counseling Psychology graduate students. After graduating from CSPP and completing NIMH post-doctral fellowship at the University of California San Francisco Medical Center he took two years of extramural training at the Cognitive Therapy Center of Philadelphia with Aaron T. Beck, M.D. He maintains a private practice in Fremont, California and serves as Director of Psychological Services at Fremont Hospital where he developed its inpatient CBT program and manual. In the beginning he earned a Masters of Divinity at the Pacific School of Religion where he studied with Rollo May, Ph.D. Dr. White currently lives in the San Francisco Bay Area with his wife and three children.